Poverty and
the Homeless

Poverty and
the Homeless

Other books in the Current Controversies series:

Poverty and the Homeless

Mary E. Williams, *Book Editor*

Bruce Glassman, *Vice President*
Bonnie Szumski, *Publisher*
Scott Barbour, *Managing Editor*
Helen Cothran, *Senior Editor*

CURRENT CONTROVERSIES

GREENHAVEN
PRESS ®

THOMSON
─────★─────
GALE

San Diego • Detroit • New York • San Francisco • Cleveland
New Haven, Conn. • Waterville, Maine • London • Munich

© 2004 by Greenhaven Press. Greenhaven Press is an imprint of The Gale Group, Inc.,
a division of Thomson Learning, Inc.

Greenhaven® and Thomson Learning™ are trademarks used herein under license.

For more information, contact
Greenhaven Press
27500 Drake Rd.
Farmington Hills, MI 48331-3535
Or you can visit our Internet site at http://www.gale.com

Cover credit: © Getty Images

LIBRARY OF CONGRESS CATALOGING-IN-PUBLICATION DATA

Poverty and the homeless / Mary E. Williams, book editor.
    p. cm. — (Current controversies)
Includes bibliographical references and index.
ISBN 0-7377-2311-4 (pbk. : alk. paper) — ISBN 0-7377-2310-6 (lib. : alk. paper)
    1. Homelessness—United States. 3. Poverty—United States. I. Williams, Mary E.,
1960– . II. Series.
HV4505.P68 2004
362.5'0973—dc22
                                                                    2003060012

Printed in the United States of America

Contents

Chapter 1: Are Poverty and Homelessness Serious Problems?

Yes: The Problems of Poverty and Homelessness Are Serious

Poverty, wage inequities, public service cutbacks, and opportunity gaps
are rampant in the United States. The working poor and the underprivi-
leged bear the brunt of budget cuts while wealthy households and corporations reap increasing profits.

Homelessness is becoming more widespread in the United States as the
availability of affordable housing decreases. Discrimination and cultural
insensitivity among service agencies often exacerbate problems for poor
people—the majority of whom are minorities—seeking assistance.

The working poor face many struggles, including a lack of affordable
housing, little or no health care, poor work conditions, and disrespectful
management at their workplaces. Entry-level workers often have to take
more than one job just to make ends meet.

No: Poverty and Homelessness Are in Decline

Since the enactment of welfare reform in the 1990s, child poverty has
declined. This decrease has been most dramatic among black children,
Hispanic children, and children in single-mother families.

Life for low-wage workers is not as grueling as some analysts have
claimed. Most employees see low-wage entry-level positions as a means
of learning the skills that will enable them to find higher-paying jobs in
the future.

Chapter 2: What Causes Poverty and Homelessness?

Chapter 3: Has Welfare Reform Helped the Poor?

increase employment and reduce poverty among single mothers and their children. Government aid has been redirected to single parents with low-wage jobs, increasing the number of resources available to needy families.

No: Welfare Reform Has Not Helped the Poor

Chapter 4: What Strategies Would Benefit the Poor and the Homeless?

mothers get married to improve their economic situations is untenable because it addresses neither the causes of poverty nor the fact that there are few men available for these women to marry.

Foreword

By definition, controversies are "discussions of questions in which opposing opinions clash" (Webster's Twentieth Century Dictionary Unabridged). Few would deny that controversies are a pervasive part of the human condition and exist on virtually every level of human enterprise. Controversies transpire between individuals and among groups, within nations and between nations. Controversies supply the grist necessary for progress by providing challenges and challengers to the status quo. They also create atmospheres where strife and warfare can flourish. A world without controversies would be a peaceful world; but it also would be, by and large, static and prosaic.

The Series' Purpose

The purpose of the Current Controversies series is to explore many of the social, political, and economic controversies dominating the national and international scenes today. Titles selected for inclusion in the series are highly focused and specific. For example, from the larger category of criminal justice, Current Controversies deals with specific topics such as police brutality, gun control, white collar crime, and others. The debates in Current Controversies also are presented in a useful, timeless fashion. Articles and book excerpts included in each title are selected if they contribute valuable, long-range ideas to the overall debate. And wherever possible, current information is enhanced with historical documents and other relevant materials. Thus, while individual titles are current in focus, every effort is made to ensure that they will not become quickly outdated. Books in the Current Controversies series will remain important resources for librarians, teachers, and students for many years.

In addition to keeping the titles focused and specific, great care is taken in the editorial format of each book in the series. Book introductions and chapter prefaces are offered to provide background material for readers. Chapters are organized around several key questions that are answered with diverse opinions representing all points on the political spectrum. Materials in each chapter include opinions in which authors clearly disagree as well as alternative opinions in which authors may agree on a broader issue but disagree on the possible solutions. In this way, the content of each volume in Current Controversies mirrors the mosaic of opinions encountered in society. Readers will quickly realize that there are many viable answers to these complex issues. By questioning each author's conclusions, students and casual readers can begin to develop the critical thinking skills so important to evaluating opinionated material.

Current Controversies is also ideal for controlled research. Each anthology in the series is composed of primary sources taken from a wide gamut of informational categories including periodicals, newspapers, books, United States and foreign government documents, and the publications of private and public organizations. Readers will find factual support for reports, debates, and research papers covering all areas of important issues. In addition, an annotated table of contents, an index, a book and periodical bibliography, and a list of organizations to contact are included in each book to expedite further research.

Perhaps more than ever before in history, people are confronted with diverse and contradictory information. During the Persian Gulf War, for example, the public was not only treated to minute-to-minute coverage of the war, it was also inundated with critiques of the coverage and countless analyses of the factors motivating U.S. involvement. Being able to sort through the plethora of opinions accompanying today's major issues, and to draw one's own conclusions, can be a complicated and frustrating struggle. It is the editors' hope that Current Controversies will help readers with this struggle.

Greenhaven Press anthologies primarily consist of previously published material taken from a variety of sources, including periodicals, books, scholarly journals, newspapers, government documents, and position papers from private and public organizations. These original sources are often edited for length and to ensure their accessibility for a young adult audience. The anthology editors also change the original titles of these works in order to clearly present the main thesis of each viewpoint and to explicitly indicate the opinion presented in the viewpoint. These alterations are made in consideration of both the reading and comprehension levels of a young adult audience. Every effort is made to ensure that Greenhaven Press accurately reflects the original intent of the authors included in this anthology.

Introduction

A crack cocaine dependency makes it difficult for forty-two-year-old Stella Tate to keep a job, pay rent, or maintain stable relationships. Consequently, Tate—who also suffers from arthritis, heart problems, and seizures—has spent several years living on the streets. During these years, she would sleep under park benches, covering herself with discarded newspapers to stay warm and hidden. On colder nights she might venture into an emergency shelter, which offered heat, but which also required her to engage in the "one-eyed sleep"—a state of half-alertness prompted by the fear of having one's possessions stolen. Tate has also been severely beaten both in the shelters and in the city parks. Presently, a rehabilitation program has helped Tate to remain drug-free for several months, and she lives in an apartment. But she is wary of taking her current life for granted. "This is not my first time rising," she admits, recalling past bouts of being sober and housed. "Raw existence can be only a few slips away."

David Christian, a rental car mechanic in his mid-thirties, lost his job when the tourist industry plummeted after the terrorist attacks of September 11, 2001. His wife Gina, a temporary worker at a nursing home, did not make enough money to support David and their four children. The family pawned off nearly everything they owned to move to Dallas, Texas, where David's former boss opened a new business. When that business failed, David and Gina had to sell parts from their two cars to pay for food. "I was reduced to begging. I felt degraded, like I was less than human," recalls Gina. Unable to pay rent, the family eventually found shelter at the Interfaith House, which provides three months' free housing for one hundred needy families each year. David now has an $8.00-per-hour job at a Texaco station, and the family has begun to save some money. But the Interfaith House has had to break its own rule and allow the family to remain for an additional three months. Otherwise they would be living in a car.

Stella Tate is the type of person many people picture when they hear the word *homeless*. Transients who are substance abusers, mentally ill, or very sick—often referred to as the "chronic homeless"—may spend years in a recurring cycle of illness, deepening poverty, institutionalization, rehabilitation attempts, and homelessness. Some remain transients for life. The chronic homeless, however, make up only 10 percent of the homeless population. Increasingly, families like David and Gina Christian and their children are joining the ranks of the destitute. An economic recession, stagnant wages, layoffs, and rising unemployment coupled with skyrocketing housing prices are pushing more and more working families onto the streets or into temporary shelters. In many cities the number of homeless families is the highest that analysts have seen in a decade. There were nine thousand homeless families in New York City in 2003—an increase of 40 percent since 2002. In Anchorage, Alaska, families made up seventeen hundred people seeking shelter in 2001—an increase of 17 percent since the year 2000. "It's embarrassing to say that the [numbers of homeless are] up," says Philip Mangano, head of the U.S. government's Interagency Council on Homelessness. "But it's better to face the truth than to try to obfuscate."

Despite the increase in homelessness, the public today does not seem to view it as a compelling social problem. In the 1980s and early 1990s, when fighting homelessness had become a popular cause, many cities built emergency shelters and supportive housing projects with on-site services for the jobless, the ill, and the addicted. But after Congress cut the budget for homeless services in the late 1990s, cities were not able to keep up with the requests for assistance, and the homeless again poured out onto the streets. Irritated with federal unresponsiveness to the homeless problem, the public at large demanded that the streets be "cleaned up." Many locales then focused on discouraging transience and keeping homeless people away from downtown areas. Orlando, Florida, for example, passed an ordinance that made it illegal to lie down on the sidewalk. An ad campaign in Philadelphia, Pennsylvania, asked people to stop giving money to panhandlers. And Santa Monica, California, adopted a law preventing transients from sleeping in shop doors or receiving food from unlicensed providers.

Another factor bearing on the perception of homelessness, according to some analysts, is the basic lack of national leadership and discussion on poverty issues. In the opinion of researcher and author Jack Newfield, "the increasing gap between rich and poor . . . are not hot-button talk-show issues because so few politicians with a national following agitate about them with continuing conviction." Moreover, Newfield points out, "[the] growing concentration of wealth has given the superrich domination over politics through extravagant campaign contributions and media ownership." He believes that the control of politics and media by the affluent makes it exceedingly difficult for the poor to be heard. Unwilling to alienate the wealthy individuals and corporations that donate to their campaigns, most major politicians avoid discussing the unequal distribution of wealth and the growth of poverty and homelessness, claims Newfield.

Susan Baker, co-chair of the National Alliance to End Homelessness, would likely disagree with Newfield's assertions about the politics of poverty. In 2001 Baker met with Housing and Urban Development (HUD) Secretary Mel Martinez to discuss solutions to homelessness. Baker had come across a new study suggesting that the best way to reduce homelessness was to provide permanent housing for the chronic homeless—the substance abusers and the very ill who are often lifelong transients. Since the long-term homeless take up 50 percent of the relatively expensive space in emergency shelters, Baker thought that providing permanent housing for them would save money and create more temporary-shelter space for homeless families. She convinced Martinez that the Bush administration could end chronic homelessness in ten years by providing 200,000 apartments for long-term transients. Since her meeting with Martinez, this "permanent housing" plan has become President George W. Bush's official stance on homelessness, and he has promised to end long-term homelessness in a decade.

But many experts believe that Bush's adopted stance does not go far enough, especially in light of the relatively small amount of new funding—$35 million—that the permanent housing plan will receive. "To give a sense of how much that means," explains *Time* reporter Joel Stein, "$35 million is equal to the money set aside to help keep insects from crossing the border." Donald Whitehead, executive director of the National Coalition for the Homeless, argues that Bush's plan is too limited: "The largest-growing sector [of the homeless] is actually women and children. A true strategy needs to include the entire population." Moreover, many advocates for the homeless contend that the new plan seems more geared to keeping the obviously homeless out of sight than in providing destitute people with assistance.

An effective strategy to help the homeless, argues Homes for the Homeless president Ralph da Costa Nunez, should focus on getting more shelters to provide supportive services for homeless individuals and families. The U.S. government, he contends, is not likely to construct enough low-income housing in the near future, and homeless people are increasingly turning to the shelter system "as the one remaining element of a dwindling safety net." But it is just this element that could begin to turn the tide of homelessness, states Nunez: "By using the national shelter infrastructure already in place . . . we can enhance services to be comprehensive and focused on building long-term skills that foster independence and economic viability." Such service-oriented shelters could provide homeless people opportunities to receive counseling, improve literacy skills, complete high school, and build an employment history. In Nunez' view, "We are going to have to acknowledge that, for the time being, a shelter is indeed a home, and one that must continue to evolve into a community with opportunities."

While analysts and policy makers differ on which strategies would best reduce destitution and homelessness, they generally agree that the persistence of poverty presents a compelling challenge that should not be ignored. In *Poverty and the Homeless: Current Controversies*, authors examine the severity of U.S. poverty and homelessness, debate the problem's root causes, and discuss various approaches to helping the poor. These chapters offer a thought-provoking introduction to the plight of America's often-invisible population of poor and homeless people.

Chapter 1

Are Poverty and Homelessness Serious Problems?

Chapter Preface

During the 1990s the United States experienced an economic boom that was accompanied by a slow decrease in the poverty rate. However, recent census data reveals that the poverty rate began rising again in the year 2001. By the year 2003, 11.7 percent of the U.S. population—32.9 million people—were living below the poverty level.

The poverty level, which is refigured annually, is defined by family size and total household income. A U.S. family is deemed "poor" if its yearly income falls below the "basic needs" level of approximately $14,100 for a three-person family, $18,400 for a four-person family, and $21,000 for a five-person family. Some analysts, however, maintain that the formula for determining these figures is so outdated that it greatly underestimates the true poverty rate. According to Lawrence Aber, executive director of Columbia University's National Center for Children in Poverty, "The poverty line isn't an adequate threshold to measure a family's economic hardship. Once you get above the poverty line, you're still very far away from economic self-sufficiency." In Aber's opinion, poverty level incomes would have to be doubled, at the very least, for most families to meet their minimum needs.

Underestimating the poverty rate creates additional difficulties for the poor, Aber and others point out, because policies and public services guided by an erroneous measurement of poverty are ineffective and even detrimental. For example, in New York City, more than six hundred thousand workers earn between $5.15 an hour (the minimum wage in 2003) and $10.00 an hour. Full-time minimum wage jobs pay less than $11,000 annually and could only sustain one worker and one dependent child at the poverty level. Yet even those who earn $10.00 an hour—living just above the official poverty level—struggle to make ends meet. According to researcher Jack Newfield, "Some 56 percent of these low-wage workers have no health insurance for their families, 32 percent have no pension plan and 37 percent receive no paid leave." Between 2002 and 2003, Newfield states, "27 percent of these workers fell behind in rent payments, 18 percent had their utilities shut off and 14 percent had to postpone necessary medical treatment." Moreover, hunger and homelessness have increased among the city's working poor—but there has been no corresponding increase in shelters, soup kitchens, and food pantries. Thus, reports the Coalition Against Hunger, in 2001 New York soup kitchens and food pantries had to turn away 350,000 people—including eighty-five thousand children. The official poverty level, many analysts contend, denies the true scope of poverty and homelessness and contributes to a disturbing neglect of the poor.

However, other experts maintain that the official poverty line actually overestimates the extent of poverty in the United States. These experts highlight the distinction between relative and absolute measures of poverty. While the relative measure defines what percentage of a population lives below a certain national level of income, the absolute measure examines what goods people can buy with their money. According to these absolute measures, poor Americans have a much higher standard of living than people of comparable incomes in other developed nations. As journalist Fidelis Iyebote points out, "Cars are owned by 70 percent of 'poor' [U.S.] households. . . . Color televisions belong to 97 percent of the 'poor' [and] videocassette recorders belong to nearly 75 percent. . . . Sixty-four percent [of the poor] have microwave ovens, half own a stereo system, and over a quarter possess an automatic dishwasher." According to Heritage Foundation poverty analyst Robert Rector, the absolute measure of poverty reveals that America has one of the lowest poverty rates among industrialized nations. "A close look at the actual material living conditions of persons defined as poor demonstrates that the Census Bureau's official poverty report is misleading," Rector states. "Real material hardship does occur," he contends, "but is limited in extent and severity."

Although census data suggests that the population of America's poor and homeless is increasing, analysts and policy makers continue to disagree about the definition of poverty and the scope of economic hardship in such an affluent nation. The authors in the following chapter provide further discussion and debate on the issue of poverty and homelessness in the United States.

Poverty and Inequality Are Serious Problems in the United States

by Holly Sklar

About the author: *Holly Sklar is the coauthor of* Raise the Floor: Wages and Policies That Work for All of Us.

Imagine a country where one out of five children is born into poverty and wealth is being redistributed upward. Since the 1970s, the top 1 percent of households has doubled their share of the nation's wealth. The top 1 percent has close to 40 percent of the wealth—nearly the same amount as the bottom 95 percent of households.

Imagine a country where economic inequality is going back to the future circa the 1930s. The combined after-tax income of the top 1 percent of tax filers was about half that of the bottom 50 percent of tax filers in 1986. By the late 1990s, the top 1 percent had a larger share of after-tax income than the bottom 50 percent.

Imagine a country with a greed surplus and justice deficit.

Imagine a country where the poor and middle class bear the brunt of severe cutbacks in education, health, environmental programs, and other public services to close state and federal budget deficits fueled by ballooning tax giveaways for wealthy households and corporations.

It's not Argentina.

Wage Inequities

Imagine a country which demands that people work for a living while denying many a living wage.

Imagine a country where health care aides can't afford health insurance. Where people working in the food industry depend on food banks to help feed their children. Where childcare teachers don't make enough to save for their own children's education.

It's not the Philippines.

Imagine a country where productivity went up, but workers' wages went down.

In the words of the national labor department, "As the productivity of workers increases, one would expect worker compensation [wages and benefits] to experience similar gains." That's not what happened.

Since 1968, worker productivity has risen 81 percent while the average hourly wage barely budged, adjusting for inflation, and the real value of the minimum wage dropped 38 percent.

> *"Millions of workers make wages so low they have to choose between eating or heating, health care or childcare."*

Imagine a country where the minimum wage just doesn't add up. Where minimum wage workers earn more than a third less than their counterparts earned a third of a century ago, adjusting for inflation. Where a couple with two children would have to work more than three full-time jobs at the $5.15 minimum wage to make ends meet.

It's not Mexico.

Imagine a country where some of the worst CEOs make millions more in a year than the best CEOs of earlier generations made in their lifetimes. CEOs made 45 times the pay of average production and nonsupervisory workers in 1980. They made 96 times as much in 1990, 160 times as much in 1995 and 369 times as much in 2001. Back in 1960, CEOs made an average 38 times more than schoolteachers. CEOs made 63 times as much in 1990 and 264 times as much as public schoolteachers in 2001.

Imagine a country that had a record-breaking ten-year economic expansion in 1991–2001, but millions of workers make wages so low they have to choose between eating or heating, health care or childcare.

A leading business magazine observed, "People who worked hard to make their companies competitive are angry at the way the profits are distributed. They think it is unfair, and they are right."

It's not England.

Falling Living Standards

Imagine a country where living standards are falling for younger generations despite increased education. Since 1973, the share of workers without a high school degree has fallen by half. The share of workers with at least a four-year college degree has doubled. But the 2002 average hourly wage for production and nonsupervisory workers (the majority of the workforce) is 7.5 percent below 1973, adjusting for inflation. Median net worth (assets minus debt) dropped between 1995 and 2001 for households headed by persons under age 35 and households that don't own their own home.

About one out of four workers makes $8.70 an hour or less. That's not much more than the real value of the minimum wage of 1968 at $8.27 in inflation-adjusted dollars.

It's not Russia.

Imagine a country where for more and more people a job doesn't keep you out of poverty, it keeps you working poor. Imagine a country much richer than it was 25 years ago, but the percentage of full-time workers living in poverty has jumped 50 percent.

Imagine a country that sets the official poverty line well below the actual cost of minimally adequate housing, health care, food, and other necessities. You were not counted as poor in 2001 (latest available final data) unless you had pre-tax incomes below these thresholds: $9,214 for a person under 65, $8,494 for a person 65 and older, $11,569 for a two-person family, $14,128 for a three-person family, and $18,104 for a family of four. On average, households need more than double the official poverty threshold to meet basic needs.

Imagine a country where homelessness is on the rise, but federal funding for low-income housing is about 50 percent lower than it was in 1976, adjusting for inflation. The largest federal housing support program is the mortgage interest deduction, which disproportionately benefits higher-income families.

> *"Homelessness is on the rise, but federal funding for low-income housing is about 50 percent lower than it was in 1976."*

Imagine a country where more workers are going back to the future of sweatshops and day labor. Corporations are replacing full-time jobs with disposable "contingent workers." They include temporary employees, contract workers, and "leased" employees—some of them fired and then "rented" back at a large discount by the same company—and involuntary part-time workers, who want permanent full-time work.

It's not Spain.

How do workers increasingly forced to migrate from job to job, at low and variable wage rates, without health insurance or paid vacation, much less a pension, care for themselves and their families, pay for college, save for retirement, plan a future, build strong communities?

Corporate Profiteering

Imagine a country where after mass layoffs and union busting, just 13.5 percent of workers are unionized. One out of three workers were union members in 1955. Full-time workers who were union members had median 2001 weekly earnings of $718 compared with just $575 for workers not represented by unions.

Imagine a country where the concerns of working people are dismissed as "special interests" and the profit-making interests of globetrotting corporations substitute for the "national interest."

Imagine a country negotiating "free trade" agreements that help corporations trade freely on cheap labor at home and abroad.

One ad financed by the country's agency for international development showed a Salvadoran woman in front of a sewing machine. It told corporations, "You can hire her for 33 cents an hour. Rosa is more than just colorful. She and her co-workers are known for their industriousness, reliability and quick learning. They make El Salvador one of the best buys." The country that financed the ad intervened militarily to make sure El Salvador would stay a "best buy" for corporations.

It's not Canada.

Gender Discrimination

Imagine a country where nearly two-thirds of women with children under age 6 and more than three-fourths of women with children ages 6–17 are in the labor force, but affordable childcare and after-school programs are scarce. Apparently, kids are expected to have three parents: Two parents with jobs to pay the bills, and another parent to be home in mid-afternoon when school lets out—as well as all summer.

Imagine a country where women working full time earn 76 cents for every dollar men earn. Women don't pay 76 cents on a man's dollar for their education, rent, food or childcare. The gender wage gap has closed just 12 cents since 1955, when women earned 64 cents for every dollar earned by men. There's still another 24 cents to go. . . .

Imagine a country where discrimination against women is pervasive from the bottom to the top of the pay scale and it's not because women are on the "mommy track." In the words of a leading business magazine, "At the same level of management, the typical woman's pay is lower than her male colleague's—even when she has the exact same qualifications, works just as many years, relocates just as often, provides the main financial support for her family, takes no time off for personal reasons, and wins the same number of promotions to comparable jobs."

Imagine a country where instead of rooting out discrimination, many policy makers are busily blaming women for their disproportionate poverty. If women earned as much as similarly qualified men, poverty in single-mother households would be cut in half.

"More workers are going back to the future of sweatshops and day labor."

It's not Japan.

Imagine a country where the awful labeling of children as "illegitimate" has again been legitimized. Besides meaning born out of wedlock, illegitimate also means illegal, contrary to rules and logic, misbegotten, not genuine, wrong—to be a bastard. The word illegitimate has consequences. It helps make people more disposable. Single mothers and their children have become prime scapegoats for illegitimate economics. . . .

Education, Race, and Income

Imagine a country whose school system is rigged in favor of the already privileged, with lower caste children tracked by race and income into the most deficient and demoralizing schools and classrooms. Public school budgets are heavily determined by private property taxes, allowing higher income districts to spend much more than poor ones. In the state with the largest gap in 1999–2000, state and local spending per pupil in districts with the lowest child poverty rates was more than $2,152 greater than districts with the highest child poverty rates. The difference amounts to about $861,000 for a typical elementary school of 400 students—money that could be used for teachers, books, and other resources. Disparities are even wider among states, with spending in districts with enrollments of 15,000 or more ranging from $3,932 per pupil in one district to $14,244 in another.

In rich districts kids take well-stocked libraries, laboratories, and state-of-the-art computers for granted. In poor schools they are rationing out-of-date textbooks and toilet paper. Rich schools often look like country clubs—with manicured sports fields and swimming pools. Poor schools often look more like jails—with concrete grounds and grated windows. College prep courses, art, music, physical education, field trips, and foreign languages are often considered necessities for the affluent, luxuries for the poor.

> *"Many policy makers are busily blaming women for their disproportionate poverty."*

Wealthier citizens argue that lack of money isn't the problem in poorer schools—family values are—until proposals are made to make school spending more equitable. Then money matters greatly for those who already have more.

It's not India.

Imagine a country whose constitution once counted black slaves as worth three-fifths of whites. Today, black per capita income is about three-fifths of whites.

Imagine a country where racial disparities take their toll from birth to death. The black infant mortality rate is more than double that of whites. Black life expectancy is nearly six years less. Black unemployment is more than twice that of whites and the black poverty rate is almost triple that of whites.

Imagine a country where the government subsidized decades of segregated suburbanization for whites while the inner cities left to people of color were treated as outsider cities—separate, unequal, and disposable. Recent studies have documented continuing discrimination in education, employment, banking, insurance, housing, and health care.

It's not South Africa.

Imagine a country where the typical non-Hispanic white household has seven times as much net worth (including home equity) as the typical household of color. From 1995 to 2001, the typical white household's net worth rose from $88,500 to $120,900 while the net worth of the typical household of color fell from $18,300 to $17,100.

> *"Black unemployment is more than twice that of whites and the black poverty rate is almost triple that of whites."*

Imagine a country that doesn't count you as unemployed just because you're unemployed. To be counted in the official unemployment rate you must have searched for work in the past four weeks. The government doesn't count people as "unemployed" if they are so discouraged from long and fruitless job searches they have given up looking. It doesn't count as "unemployed" those who couldn't look for work in the past month because they had no childcare, for example. If you need a full-time job, but you're working part-time—whether 1 hour or 34 hours weekly—because that's all you can find, you're counted as employed.

A leading business magazine observed, "Increasingly the labor market is filled with surplus workers who are not being counted as unemployed."

It's not Germany. . . .

The Cycle of Unequal Opportunity

Imagine a country where the cycle of unequal opportunity is intensifying. Its beneficiaries often slander those most systematically undervalued, underpaid, underemployed, underfinanced, underinsured, underrated, and otherwise underserved and undermined—as undeserving, "underclass," impoverished in moral and social values, and lacking the proper "work ethic." The oft-heard stereotype of deadbeat poor people masks the growing reality of dead-end jobs and disposable workers.

Imagine a country that abolished aid to families with dependent children while maintaining aid for dependent corporations.

Imagine a country where state and local governments are rushing to expand lotteries, video poker, and other government-promoted gambling to raise revenues, disproportionately from the poor, which they should be raising from a fair tax system.

Imagine a country whose military budget tops average Cold War levels although the break up of the Soviet Union produced friends, not foes. This nation spends almost as much on the military as the rest of the world combined and leads the world in arms exports.

Imagine a country that ranks first in the world in wealth and military power, and 34th in child mortality (under five), tied with Malaysia and well behind countries such as Singapore and South Korea. If the government were a parent it would be guilty of child abuse. Thousands of children die preventable deaths.

Imagine a country where health care is managed for healthy profit. In many countries health care is a right, but in this nation one out of six people under age 65 has no health insurance, public or private.

Healthcare is literally a matter of life and death. Lack of health insurance typically means lack of preventive health care and delayed or second-rate treatment. The uninsured are at much higher risk for chronic disease and disability, and have a 25 percent greater chance of dying (adjusting for physical, economic, and behavioral factors). Uninsured women are 49 percent more likely to die than women with insurance during the four to seven years following an initial diagnosis of breast cancer.

Imagine a country where many descendants of its first inhabitants live on reservations strip-mined of natural resources and have a higher proportion of people in poverty than any other ethnic group.

Imagine a country where 500 years of plunder and lies are masked in expressions like "Indian giver." Where the military still dubs enemy territory, "Indian country.". . .

The Blame Game

Imagine a country where white men who are "falling down" the economic ladder are being encouraged to believe they are falling because women and people of color are climbing over them to the top or dragging them down from the bottom. That way, they will blame women and people of color rather than corporate and government policy. They will buy the myth of "reverse discrimination." Never mind that white males hold most senior management positions and continuing unreversed discrimination is well documented.

Imagine a country with a president [George W. Bush] who, even more than his father before him, "was born on third base and thought he hit a triple." The president wants to undo affirmative action. Never mind that despite all his advantages he was a mediocre student who relied on legacy affirmative action for the children of rich alumni to get into a top prep school and college. Never mind that he rode his family connections in business and politics.

> *"Imagine a country that abolished aid to families with dependent children while maintaining aid for dependent corporations."*

Imagine a country where on top of discrimination comes insult. It's common for people of color to get none of the credit when they succeed—portrayed as undeserving beneficiaries of affirmative action and "reverse discrimination"—and all of the blame when they fail. . . .

It's not Italy.

It's the United States.

Decades ago Martin Luther King Jr. called on us to take the high road in *Where Do We Go from Here: Chaos or Community?* King wrote: "A true revolution of values will soon cause us to question the fairness and justice of many of our past and present policies. We are called to play the good Samaritan on life's roadside; but . . . one day the whole Jericho road must be transformed so that men and women will not be beaten and robbed as they make their journey through life. . . .

"A true revolution of values will soon look uneasily on the glaring contrast of poverty and wealth. . . . There is nothing but a lack of social vision to prevent us from paying an adequate wage to every American citizen whether he be a hospital worker, laundry worker, maid or day laborer. There is nothing except short-sightedness to prevent us from guaranteeing an annual minimum—and livable—income for every American family."

Homelessness Is a Serious Problem

by Silja J.A. Talvi

About the author: *Silja J.A. Talvi is a Seattle, Washington–based freelance journalist.*

When Mikala Berbery, an African American woman and single mother, went from earning $21,000 a year to losing her job, her life suddenly plunged into a dangerous abyss of homelessness.

Altogether, Berbery spent two and a half years of her life in the Boston area without a home to call her own, struggling to find shelter for herself and her young son. The seemingly insurmountable challenges she faced trying to climb out of the "hole" of homelessness, explains Berbery, often left her feeling hopeless and despondent over her future.

Yet Berbery was determined not to end up sleeping on the streets and to keep her son in school. She applied for subsidized transitional housing, but was promptly denied because she had found a job working 20 hours a week, earning just $8 an hour, income considered high enough to warrant a rejection of her application. As a last resort, Berbery moved into a run-down, $65-per-week rooming house with her son. The battles continued every step of the way.

When Berbery took the next step and applied for federally subsidized Section 8 housing after losing her part-time job, she was told she wasn't eligible because she was considered "housed." But Berbery wouldn't take the situation lying down, and fought for her right to be granted Section 8 housing. On appeal, she won.

"Five years later, I'm still digging out of the trench [of homelessness]," says Berbery, who now works as the coordinator of Boston-based organization Roofless Women, devoted to the issues of low-income and homeless women. "I worry about getting old and what's going to happen to me . . . I don't have 'bling-bling' champagne dreams; I'm just worried about having a place where I can go to the bathroom and brush my teeth."

Homelessness in America

Berbery's concerns about long-term housing prospects are shared by the estimated 31 million Americans who lived in an "official" state of poverty in 2000. According to the U.S. Census, a total of 49 million Americans, or roughly one in five people, lived in a household in 2000 that had difficulty meeting basic needs. Most disturbingly, at least three million American men, women and children fell so deeply into poverty—or other difficult life circumstances—that they ended up homeless at some point in the past year [2001–2002].

America's homeless population is anything but monolithic. Surveys of major urban centers reveal that roughly 20 percent of the homeless hold down regular jobs, and that 40 percent are families with children.

> *"At least three million American men, women and children fell so deeply into poverty . . . that they ended up homeless at some point in the past year."*

The demographics of homelessness have also taken on a significant dimension that is often omitted from the realm of public policy and media coverage: Put simply, people of color represent the majority of the homeless in the nation.

In a December 2001 report released by the U.S. Conference of Mayors, data from 27 cities rallied the nation's homeless population at 50 percent African American, 12 percent Latino, 2 percent Native American and 1 percent Asian American.

"I think of homelessness as a game of musical chairs, where people are competing for scarce resources like affordable housing," says Timothy Harris, director of Seattle's Real Change Homeless Empowerment Project. "People who lose in that game are those who have the odds stacked against them . . . and race is one of those variables."

No Job, No House, Facing Jail

. . . Before becoming homeless, Berbery recalls, she spent three weeks looking at 30 apartments. With her modest salary, Berbery found only one apartment complex she could afford, and where the managers were willing to let her and her son move in. The color of her skin, says Berbery, compounded the problem of trying to find housing in a largely white suburb of Boston. "You just know," she explains. "You know when that's the thing that's keeping you from getting an apartment."

But, as Berbery readily admits, housing discrimination is a hard thing to prove. In lending practices, for instance, the most recent Fannie Mae National Housing Survey showed that 39 percent of African Americans believe that they suffer from discrimination in obtaining mortgages "all or most of the time," but only a small fraction of these cases ever result in formal complaints.

In addition, low-income people are confronted with soaring housing costs and tight rental markets nationwide. A recent national survey from the National Low Income Housing Coalition (NLIHC) revealed that nowhere in the U.S. can a minimum wage worker afford fair market rental costs for a modest two-bedroom housing unit. In order to afford the median fair market rent for a two-bedroom rental unit, a worker would have to earn $13.87 per hour, or 269 percent of the federal minimum wage. (In 2000, roughly 2.7 million Americans earned minimum wage which, on a federal level, has remained at $5.15 since 1997.)

Simultaneously, the number of housing units affordable to low-income households has dropped, year by year. According to a 2001 HUD [Housing and Urban Development] report, 1.14 million affordable housing units were lost between 1997 and 1999.

"The reality is that there's a persistent and extensive gap between earnings at the low end of the wage scale and basic housing costs," says Sheila Crowley, executive director of NLIHC. "And rental rates aren't going to go down in the near future because there's still a severe shortage of housing [along with] high demand for housing."

As of January 2002, the U.S. unemployment rate remained high at 5.6 percent, not including the ranks of the homeless or the incarcerated. According to the Bureau of Labor Statistics, unemployment continued to be most pronounced among African Americans (9.8 percent) and Latinos (8.1 percent).

> *"[Eighty] percent of . . . rural and urban jurisdictions . . . [criminalize] homelessness by banning public sleeping or camping."*

[After the terrorist attacks of September 11, 2001], large-scale layoffs have been concentrated in retail, hotel, air transport and building services industries, where many low-income workers of color have traditionally found employment.

Indio, editor of the homeless newspaper *Street News* (and a Black Cherokee Seminole who goes by only one name), says that the fallout of these layoffs is already visible in terms of the number of homeless people trying to access shelter and transitional housing services in New York City. There are now roughly 30,000 homeless adults and children in local shelters—an all-time high for New York City. And to compound matters, both the [Rudolph] Giuliani and [Michael] Bloomberg city administrations have cracked down on so-called "quality of life" hazards, seizing copies of *Street News* and arresting people for trying to make a living selling their wares or busking in subway stations.

In January 2002, a report released by the National Homeless Civil Rights Organizing Project ranked New York, Atlanta and San Francisco as the worst cities as far as harassment and arrests of homeless persons are concerned. Across the nation, 80 percent of the rural and urban jurisdictions surveyed were, in effect, criminalizing homelessness by banning public sleeping or camping. And fully 100 percent lacked enough shelter beds to meet demand.

These findings come amidst the widespread agreement that homelessness in the U.S. is becoming more widespread. The Conference of Mayors reported in December [2001] that all cities expected both food assistance and shelter requests to increase in 2002 because of the post-911 economy, the expiration of welfare and unemployment benefits, lack of affordable housing and the preponderance of low-paying jobs.

The Struggle Within

Most of the social service agencies that low-income people turn to are designed almost as a measure of last resort—places of intervention, refuge and even life-saving assistance.

But in general terms, says Larry Evans, a former gang-intervention specialist and case manager for homeless youth, "They've been designed to keep the power away from the community. [Most social service agencies] don't have enough interest in disrupting the class structure in America to put together programs that help people gain real education, training and self-understanding."

With a particular emphasis on the community that he knows personally as an African American man, Evans says, unequivocally, that a huge part of the problem is that denial about homelessness, drug use, and family dysfunction runs strong within communities of color. As "unpopular" an opinion as it is, says Evans, "one of the things that's really hurt black youth and black people in general regarding homelessness is that we haven't been addressing it ourselves. Just like other problems, we often run to others and demand that they do something about it."

African Americans who become homeless often feel invisible within their own communities. "For years, we've turned a blind eye to it," says Evans. "We act like we don't see it."

Intensifying the problem in the lives of homeless persons of color is the fact that this sense of invisibility and self-loathing can manifest in even more brutal ways. Back in New York City, for instance, *Street News* editor Indio recalls the hardship he faced as a light-skinned person of color trying to find a safe place to sleep in city shelters populated mainly by African Americans. "If you had light or 'high yella' skin,

> *"Homelessness in the U.S. is becoming more widespread."*

they would beat you up. You'd be afraid to go to sleep." Security personnel, adds Indio, often have little or no interest in controlling hostility or outright violence between the men staying in city shelters.

The problem is perhaps less overtly antagonistic between homeless women of color. But tensions may still take many forms, explains Berbery of Boston's Roofless Women, in the form of clashes between newly homeless and long-term homeless women. "There are newly homeless women out there who are looking down on other women. They separate themselves from other women saying things like, 'I never thought this would happen to me. . . . I never thought I would live like this.'

"But there are a lot of smart people out here at the bottom, and we're watching how we're being played off of each other," Berbery adds thoughtfully. "When we look at it closely, we're kicking each other and someone else is getting over."

From Jail to the Streets

At a crowded, rundown, downtown Seattle intersection, Street Outreach Services outreach worker Darrell Green waves his hand in the direction of a group of hollow-eyed men and women whom he knows to be among his drug-addicted and homeless clients. "This is misery and pain, what you see here," Green says firmly. "They never learned any other way to deal with that pain."

"Nationwide, it's estimated that 22 percent of homeless men and women grapple with mental illness."

A difficult divorce brought Green to these same streets just two years ago, where he ended up drug-addicted, strung out, slapped with a felony charge, and doing a stint in a local jail. Green's incarceration did nothing to help improve his prospects in the real world, he insists. Released from jail without access to drug treatment or counseling, Green readily admits that he went right back "to the life," dealing and using drugs as a way of coping with severe depression.

Nationwide, it's estimated that 22 percent of homeless men and women grapple with mental illness. Alcohol or chemical addiction is even more common, afflicting an estimated 34 percent of the homeless population. To compound the problem, waiting lists for publicly subsidized drug treatment can be as long as a year-and-a-half in major urban cities like Seattle, says Kris Nyrop, director of Street Outreach Services.

Because of widespread racial profiling and the uneven application of prison sentences, African Americans and Latinos now make up 62 percent of the incarcerated population, despite comprising only 25 percent of the overall population. Altogether, African American men are sent to state prisons on drug charges at 13 times the rate of white men, and constitute between 80 percent and 90 percent of all people sent to prison on drug charges.

Even in recovery, the struggles continue. Among many immediate hurdles facing homeless men and women trying to get back on their feet after incarceration is the fact that most public housing is not available to those with felony drug convictions, and employers are less likely to hire those with jail or prison records, even for nonviolent offenses.

"When a white junkie stops being a junkie, they can go back to being white," adds Nyrop. "When a black junkie stops being a junkie, he goes back to being black. In a country where race is still critically important, that's a big distinction."

Does Culture Matter?

Experts acknowledge that there are a host of overarching issues that the social service network was never designed to address.

Real Change's director Harris makes the point that most programs available to homeless persons "do not focus on the cultural needs of minority groups."

Says Harris, "In the overall mix of things, the need for social services is really desperate. . . [in terms of] mental health, drug treatment and housing. To a lot of service providers and funders, services that focus more on the cultural needs of homeless and low-income persons are not seen as being survival-oriented. They are lower on the totem pole [of social services]."

"Most public housing is not available to those with felony drug convictions."

But a handful of public and private social organizations are trying to provide the kinds of programs that make a specific difference for people of color living in dire poverty and struggling with homelessness.

The Chief Seattle Club, a 31-year-old drop-in center in downtown Seattle, operates five days a week, offering breakfast, clothing, laundry service, showers and case management to the 60–125 men and women who come to the shelter each day.

"The crushing poverty among Natives is there," says Gary Graham, director of the Chief Seattle Club. "There are huge gaps in services to Native Americans . . . and it is clear that some shelters and [agencies] seem to be more sensitive to the needs of Native Americans than others."

Graham and others who work at the agency place a priority on understanding the historical experiences and cultural etiquette of local Indian tribes, with an emphasis on one strong commonality. "Natives suffer from a kind of post-traumatic stress because of the selective holocaust that happened in this country," notes Graham, a psychologist whose passion for the welfare of Indian people stems from his own Oklahoma Cherokee heritage. "Those kinds of things have long-term effects on people."

In general, Graham says, homeless and impoverished Native Americans tend to be reticent to ask for help, so when people do reach out for housing assistance or health care, agencies would do well to learn to appreciate Indian sensibilities and cultural experiences. Among those sensibilities, says Graham, is the "tendency to go inward under times of stress."

"It's true of Native Americans and minority groups in general. If they don't trust you—and the distrust of the dominant culture is very great—they will not receive healing from you. Unfortunately, there are people who are culturally ignorant of many minority peoples, and they will inadvertently offend [them]." And when people feel condescended to, stresses Graham, there is a good chance that they will not return to seek assistance, even to the detriment of their own health or housing situation.

"We're dying like flies out there, and death is all around us," Graham remembers one young Native American man telling him at a memorial service for another urban Indian.

"We recognize that crushing poverty and homelessness are serious problems, but we also have to realize that emotional, identity and spiritual issues are also there," he adds. "These are all very powerful problems, and there's a lot yet left to be done."

Life for the Working Poor Is Exceptionally Difficult

by Barbara Ehrenreich, interviewed by *Multinational Monitor*

About the author: *Cultural critic and researcher Barbara Ehrenreich is the author of several books.* Multinational Monitor *is a monthly magazine that focuses on the issues of labor, the environment, corporate ethics, and globalization.*

Barbara Ehrenreich is the author of a number of books, including *Nickel and Dimed: On (Not) Getting By in America, Blood Rites* and *The Worst Years of Our Lives.* In *Nickel and Dimed,* she reports on her experiences trying to live on the income she earned while working at various entry-level jobs.

Multinational Monitor: What kind of ground rules did you impose upon yourself for the project that resulted in your book?

Barbara Ehrenreich: The idea was simply to see if I could make enough money to support myself as an entry-level worker. I tried this in three cities— Key West, Florida; Portland, Maine; and the Twin Cities [Minnesota] area. I stayed for a month in each city. I tried my best to get the best-paying entry-level job I could, did my best at it and kept my expenses to an absolute minimum. All of those rules were broken or twisted in some way or another along the way, but that was the idea.

Housing Problems

In the book, housing emerges as a central concern.

Yes. If I had small children with me, I'm sure childcare would have loomed just as large, but as a single person, housing was an insuperable barrier.

In the Twin Cities area, I could find nothing affordable. I discovered there and in Portland, Maine, that it's the lucky people who can get into a trailer park. Trailers are high-rent. For example, it costs $625 a month to rent a one-person trailer in the area that serves the Key West hotel industry. In Maine and Minnesota, I didn't find anything less than $800 a month.

I found that people ended up in residential hotels, which I guess are okay if you don't mind living in one little room with a kitchenette. I'm speaking now of families—for me that wasn't a problem. But some of those places were appalling, and extremely expensive. Like the creepy one I lived in for a while in Minnesota, which charged $250 a week. That was more than I was earning. It was filthy and unsafe and didn't have a kitchenette or even a microwave or a fridge.

If you had stayed in these cities longer than a month, could you have found more permanent arrangements that would have been cheaper?

It could have gone either way. Staying longer in Minnesota would have meant homelessness. I had to give up—there was nothing I could have done except go to a shelter. That was the only option. In Maine, the residential hotel was relatively inexpensive—$120 a week, which is not so inexpensive when you think of what you're getting. Since I had two jobs there, I might have been able to save enough to get the first month's rent and deposit, to get a real apartment somewhere, if nothing had gone wrong—if I hadn't had an illness or had car problems, for example.

Did your co-workers also have these kind of temporary housing arrangements?

Many did not, because they had been living in the region for some time, and had spouses or boyfriends or grown children who were also contributing to the family income. But there were certainly other people having those kinds of problems, even people who were homeless.

How did housing arrangements limit your food alternatives?

That depends on the place. Even in the best places I lived in, a lot of my plans for economical cooking went down the drain, because I lacked the pots and pans and other things I normally take for granted that enable me to make cheap food in quantity and freeze it. If you have no kitchenette, no microwave and no refrigerator, you are left to eat in convenience stores and fast food places.

What's the cost of that?

The cost was alarming. I think I got it down so I could eat for about $9 a day. I'd get my breakfast items from a convenience store, and eat fast food for lunch and dinner. I suppose you could get cheaper than that, but that was the best I could do. As for nutritional choices, I made good choices. You eat a lot of hamburgers, though.

Would you go hungry at times?

I didn't eat snacks or other things that I might have ordinarily. But no, one of the things I resolved at the beginning of the project was that I would not let myself become homeless or go hungry. There are limits to my dedication as a journalist.

Entry-Level Jobs

What was the range of jobs that you did during this stint?

I was a waitress, a hotel housekeeper, a maid with a big corporate house-cleaning service, a nursing home aide and a Wal-Mart clerk. They were all entry-level jobs. A lot of my skills were out of date. For example, my experience in waitressing was out of date. A lot of things have changed. When I first waitressed, they didn't have computerized ordering systems. Now they do almost everywhere.

I had to struggle to learn every job. It wasn't easy. I was prepared to work hard physically, but I was not prepared for how much I had to struggle to learn these jobs.

In some it was quite overwhelming, like the Wal-Mart job. I was in ladies wear. It's a very hard job, because that's where things are constantly taken off the shelves and racks and tried on or just dumped on the floor. My job was to constantly return them to their exact places, by size, color, style, etc. That meant memorizing the exact location of hundreds of items. I can't describe to you how difficult that was. The Jordache clam-diggers with the embroidered fringe—where do they go? Hundreds of items like that. Every few days those items would be rotated around to new locations because that's part of retailing. You don't have everything in the same location, because customers return and they want to be surprised.

> *"In Portland, Maine, . . . it's the lucky people who can get into a trailer park."*

So there was not a lot of daydreaming time in these jobs. It was all hard. That's why I no longer use the word "unskilled" to describe any job.

None of the jobs you did were construction work, but you encountered real physical challenges and potential for injury.

The worst job physically was the housecleaning job. Corporate housecleaning services like Merry Maids use a highly-Taylorized approach to house-cleaning. You work in a team. The work is divided up. The exact way you proceed through a room is specified and taught to you in training videos. The problem was that you were under such great time pressure. We had only so many minutes to clean a house, according to its size. We had to stay within that time—as little as 45 minutes. So we were really running. We literally ran from the company car carrying our buckets and vacuum cleaner and everything, and ran back out, and did not pause for a second when we were in the house.

At first, I was pretty proud of myself for keeping up with everyone else. A lot of them were a lot younger than me. I could carry the buckets and the backpack vacuum cleaner. But then I began to realize that I shouldn't be so proud, because the only reason I was so strong and in such good shape was because I hadn't done it for long. Even women who had been doing it for a few months had some sort of injury—back or knee or repetitive stress injuries, such as in their scrubbing arms.

No Affordable Health Care

How did the employers respond to injuries?

The boss was horrible. He lectured us. We would have these little meetings in the morning before we took off. These meetings were rather irritating, because we weren't paid to be at them. He got about a half-hour of free time from us by making us show up at 7:30 A.M., although we didn't leave to start cleaning until 8:00.

During that time, he'd lecture us on themes like, "working through it." Don't call in with a migraine. Take a couple of Excedrin. Whatever it is, you could work through it. That was one place where I broke my rule about always being a good and obedient and cheerful worker. I blew up at this boss. He was saying this to a young woman who had really hurt herself on the job.

How did the employees respond when they were injured?

When this girl hurt herself, she started crying. She was in a lot of pain and couldn't put her weight on her ankle.

I said, "We've got to get you to an emergency room. This is ridiculous, we can't go on to the next house." The other two women on the team looked at me blankly.

The one who was hurt was ambivalent. She was a team leader that day. She really wanted to work. She couldn't afford to lose a few hours of work. She would not be paid if we had gone to get medical help. The other question that hadn't entered my middle-class mind was who would pay if we went to an emergency room. I think that question was very much on her mind.

> *"If you're only making a thousand dollars a month, you don't have . . . $150 to put into health insurance."*

I lost the argument entirely, and she ended up hopping around on one foot cleaning some rich person's bathrooms. I felt as helpless as I have ever felt in my life. I knew this was wrong. I tried all kinds of things. I told her to let me do her work for the day and sit down. She refused. She couldn't afford the time off, and she was under pressure from her husband not to take time off.

Who would have paid for medical coverage? What kind of insurance was available at the jobs you had?

There was health insurance available at almost all these jobs, but most of the people I talked to didn't bother taking it because the employee contribution was too high. If you're only making a thousand dollars a month, you don't have a hundred dollars or $150 to put into health insurance.

No Leisure Time

One of the interesting themes in the book is the concept of time. Leaving aside the time on the job, how much time do the people in entry-level positions have to do what they want with the rest of their lives?

I think a lot of people don't just work 40 hours a week. I met so many people working more than one job that I really can't believe what the Bureau of Labor Statistics says—that only 6 percent of Americans work more than one job. I must have met all of them. So one big problem is that many have to work more than one job.

My life was a little odd. If I was working an eight or nine-hour shift, I still had to go home and make my notes for the day on my laptop.

Other people very frequently went home to children that needed attention, or to their own houses that needed cleaning, that sort of thing.

I didn't get a sense that people had a lot of leisure time. Just from conversations with people, very few were talking about fun things they did on the weekend. Movies were not mentioned. Weirdly enough, not even television was mentioned. Shopping was certainly not a recreational activity.

What about the issue of time on the job, and the struggle for control over time between employees and employers?

The more highly-organized employers like Wal-Mart are watching your time down to an interval that's probably less than a minute. They warn you in the beginning during your orientation about "time theft"—meaning time when you're doing anything other than working. That includes going to the bathroom during your time on the floor.

My typical shift was nine hours. There was a one-hour dinner break, because this was an evening shift, and two 10-minute breaks—one before and one after the dinner break. You had to walk all the way to the back of the store and punch out on the time clock for your 10-minute break. Then you had to punch back in. They were watching that closely. I actually engaged in time theft, in that I would go to the ladies room on my way to punch out. I don't know what problems would have ensued if I had been detected.

That ten minutes was a big deal. For a lot of people, that was time to call home and see how the kids were doing. They had pay phones in the back of the store, and people had to hope that one would be free.

I had a very strong desire to get out of doors. Nine hours is a long time to spend in a fluorescent-lit, stale-air atmosphere.

You couldn't just stand in front of the store. They had a fenced-off area that the smokers could go to. You could sit back there—there was a picnic table and so on. It was very important to be able to sit down. You had been on your feet for hours. I even begrudged the 75 seconds that it took me to walk outside from where I punched out. I wanted to be outdoors and off my feet. I needed to drink something. You don't even drink water when you're working. Sometimes I needed a snack to keep going. So you had all these things you had to do in your 10 minutes. That was also my big occasion to talk with people from other departments, which was important and interesting to me as a journalist, because break-time is the only time to talk.

Supervisors and Managers

What were your relationships like with your supervisors?

Varied. I liked my immediate supervisor at Wal-Mart very much. She was a middle-aged lady, not authoritarian. She had a lot of good ideas about how to improve our department—none of which were ever acted upon, because she had no authority herself. She was fine.

But the person above her was an asshole. He was a guy in his mid-twenties who delighted in exerting his authority. He was constantly calling us together for absolutely useless meetings. A lot of employees wouldn't even bother going, even though it was said to be mandatory. People would just sneer, "Okay you can go, Barb, if you want to go." The meetings were to give some kind of lecture or remind us of some rule.

> *"One big problem is that many have to work more than one job."*

In the restaurants, there were good supervisors who were not paid a lot themselves—maybe $20,000 a year. Some of them work very hard and understand that their role is to pitch in if we were short-handed. A manager at a restaurant should be able to cook or serve or do many other things if necessary to provide backup.

Others didn't see themselves that way and thought that their role was to sit in a booth with their feet up and watch us. Some of them were rude and harassing and abusive. I remember one manager who put her face right up to mine and yelled at me about how I wasn't being fast enough and I was talking to the customers too much. She was also really rude to the immigrant dishwashers. . . .

Worker Solidarity

To what extent are people working in support of each other or in solidarity, and to what extent do they work against each other?

As I quickly learned in each of these situations, there's a kind of structural solidarity in most jobs. You do depend on other people. I certainly did.

One of the things that made me work harder than I might have otherwise was the fear of letting down the people I was working with. If you don't hold up your end, someone else was going to have to do it, and that puts a lot of psychological pressure on you to do your best.

I saw examples of solidarity in small ways—people looking out for each other, warning each other about the particular manager on duty, or covering for each other when someone wanted to sneak off for a bathroom break.

I was also disappointed at times. In that confrontation I had with the housecleaning boss, my two other co-workers didn't seem to be behind me in doing something for the woman who was hurt. They just kind of were ready to go back to work. What is that about? It could be some kind of regional cultural thing about rural white people in Maine. I don't know. But on the whole, apart from the fact that there are intimate frictions that develop on any job, you know that you depend on each other. That kind of built-in solidarity could be the basis for confronting management and demanding a better break.

Everything would seem to point to the interests of these workers in joining to-gether formally in unions, or at least informally to stand up to some of the abuses you experienced. But it doesn't seem to happen. What is the explanation for that?

The thing that became absolutely clear to me is that the workplace is a totalitarian setting. It's an atmosphere of fear. You can be fired at will in the American workplace, unless it is unionized or you have a contract. You can be fired because you have a funny look on your face. You can certainly be fired for being a troublemaker and, although it's completely illegal, people are fired all the time for union activity. I read that the AFL-CIO estimates 10,000 people are fired or punished in some way each year for union activity. I've since been told that that's a gross underestimate, that it could be several times that. So it's fear.

I always thought that these jobs weren't worth taking any abuse—that you could walk down the street and get another, which was certainly true between 1998 and 2000 when I was doing this. But although these jobs don't pay much, what I came to appreciate is that to change jobs is to lose at least two weeks pay. That could be a crippling blow.

Child Poverty Has Decreased

by Robert E. Rector

About the author: *Robert E. Rector is a senior research fellow at the Heritage Foundation, a conservative public policy research foundation.*

Data released by the U.S. Bureau of the Census on Tuesday, September 24, [2002], show that black child poverty decreased in 2001, reaching the lowest level in U.S. history. This decline in black child poverty occurred despite the current economic recession which began in April 2001.

The Census Bureau report also shows that, despite the current economic recession, overall child poverty did not increase in 2001. The failure of child poverty to rise during a recession is highly unusual. In all previous recessionary years since the early 1960s, child poverty increased sharply. Historically, the average increase in child poverty during a recessionary year has been 1.4 percentage points. Annual increases in child poverty range from a low of 1.0 percentage point in the recession year 1990 to a high of 1.9 percentage points in both 1980 and 1982.

In past recessions, the most severe economic impact invariably has fallen on children. On average, the increase in child poverty during recessions has been twice as large as the increase in poverty among the general population. During the 2001 recession, this pattern was reversed for the first time. For example, during prior recessionary years, child poverty increased by an average of 1.4 percentage points while non-elderly adult poverty increased by only 0.6 percentage point. In 2001, child poverty remained essentially flat while non-elderly adult poverty increased significantly by 0.5 percentage point.

The typical racial impacts of a recession were also reversed in the current economic downturn. Historically, recessions have increased poverty among black and Hispanic children far more than among non-Hispanic white children. During the 2001 recession, this long-standing pattern was reversed; poverty among non-Hispanic white children increased (from 9.1 percent to 9.5 percent) while poverty among black and Hispanic children actually fell. Among black children, the poverty rate actually fell by one full percentage point from 31.2 percent to 30.2 percent.

Obviously, the recession that started in 2001 differs markedly from previous recessions. For individuals and families without children, the current recession appears to follow normal patterns. But for families with children, and minorities in particular, the current recession has clearly broken from the normal historical pattern.

The Impact of Welfare Reform

The unusual changes in poverty during 2001 can be traced back to the mid-1990s. In the early 1990s, states began to experiment with welfare reform. In 1996, Congress enacted national welfare reform, replacing the traditional Aid to Families with Dependent Children (AFDC) program with a new program called Temporary Assistance to Needy Families (TANF). Welfare reform, for the first time, required many welfare recipients either to obtain jobs or to prepare for work.

After welfare reform, child poverty began to drop at an unprecedented rate precisely among those groups most tightly linked to the welfare system: children in single-mother families, black children, and Hispanic children. Between 1995 (the last year before enactment of national reform) and 2001, poverty in each of these three groups dropped by at least 11 percentage points. For example, Hispanic child poverty fell by nearly one-third, from 40.0 percent in 1995 to 28 percent in 2001.

By contrast, poverty among groups unaffected by welfare reform declined only slightly. For example, poverty among the elderly dropped from 10.5 percent in 1995 to 10.1 percent in 2001. Poverty among non-elderly adults fell from 11.4 percent in 1995 to 10.1 percent in 2001.

Historically, non-Hispanic white children are far less likely to receive welfare than are Hispanic or black children. Consequently, these children were less affected by welfare reform. After reform, child poverty declined twice as rapidly among blacks and Hispanics as it did among non-Hispanic whites.

This pattern continued into the current recession. Groups less affected by welfare reform experienced increases in poverty, but among the groups most directly affected by reform, normal recession patterns were disrupted and poverty either remained constant or fell. . . .

"After [welfare] reform, child poverty declined twice as rapidly among blacks and Hispanics as it did among non-Hispanic whites."

The decline in poverty since welfare reform has been particularly dramatic among black children. As Chart 1 shows, for a quarter-century prior to welfare reform, there was little change in black child poverty. Black child poverty was

Chart 1. Black Child Poverty, 1970–2001

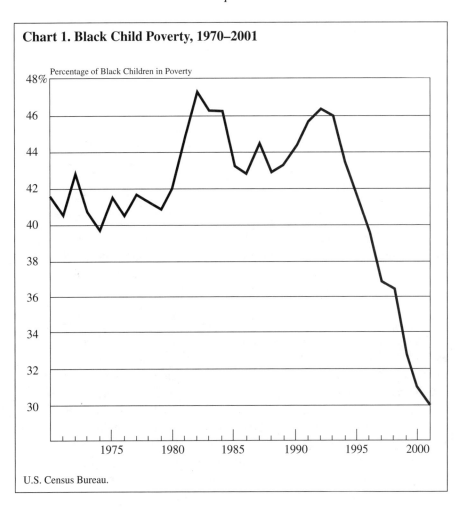

Percentage of Black Children in Poverty

U.S. Census Bureau.

actually higher in 1995 (41.5 percent) than in 1971 (40.4 percent).

With the enactment of welfare reform in 1996, black child poverty plummeted at an unprecedented rate, falling by more than a quarter to 30.2 percent in 2001. Over a six-year period after welfare reform, 1.2 million black children were lifted out of poverty. In 2001, despite the recession, the poverty rate for black children was at the lowest point in national history. . . .

Since the enactment of welfare reform, the drop in child poverty among children in single-mother families has been equally dramatic. For a quarter-century before welfare reform, there was little net decline in poverty in this group. Poverty was only slightly lower in 1995 (50.3 percent) than it had been in 1971 (53.1 percent). After the enactment of welfare reform, the poverty rate for children of single mothers fell at a dramatic rate, from 50.3 percent in 1995 to 39.3 percent in 2001. In 2001, despite the recession, the poverty rate for children in single-mother families was at the lowest point in U.S. history.

How Welfare Reform Reduced Child Poverty

The 1996 welfare reform dramatically changed the traditional welfare system. The reform required, for the first time, that welfare recipients take a job or prepare for work. As a result, the caseload in the Temporary Assistance to Needy Families program dropped by 50 percent. As welfare caseloads fell, employment of disadvantaged single mothers increased by 50 percent to 100 percent. As the employment of single mothers increased, the poverty rate in this group fell at an unprecedented rate.

> *"In 2001, despite the recession, the poverty rate for black children was at the lowest point in national history."*

Welfare reform has also kept poverty from rising in a recession. In prior recessions, single mothers have tended to leave the labor force and enroll in Aid to Families with Dependent Children. Families on welfare will, in nearly all cases, be poor. Thus, as AFDC caseloads rose, child poverty automatically increased as well.

Welfare reform created pressure for single mothers to remain in the labor force and not to enter the welfare rolls. Consequently, the increase in welfare caseloads during the current recession has been quite modest. The fact that few single mothers have left the labor force and enrolled in welfare is a significant factor in preventing the rise of child poverty during the current recession.

Welfare reform's emphasis on personal responsibility also affected family patterns. Prior to welfare reform, the out-of-wedlock birth rate increased at an alarming pace. In the mid-1960s, 7 percent of all American children were born outside marriage; by the mid-1990s, the number had risen to 32 percent. With the enactment of welfare reform, the growth of non-marital childbearing came to a near standstill. The percentage of black children living in married two-parent families also increased for the first time in a half-century. This increase in black married couples has contributed to the decline of black child poverty.

Opposition to Welfare Reform

The current good economic news about child poverty clashes strongly with the dire predictions made by opponents of welfare reform. When welfare reform was enacted in 1996, opponents predicted it would lead to dramatic increases in child poverty even in good economic times. The Children's Defense Fund claimed that welfare reform would cast millions of children into poverty and hunger. The Urban Institute predicted that the welfare law would cause the incomes of one out of 10 American families to fall and throw 1.1 million children into poverty.

Obviously, these predictions were inaccurate. The exact opposite occurred. In 1995, prior to reform, 14.7 million children lived in poverty; by 2001, the number of poor children had fallen to 11.7 million. Thus, in 2001, there were nearly

3 million fewer children in poverty than there had been before the reform. Similarly, the child poverty rate fell from a pre-reform level of 20.8 percent in 1995 to 16.3 percent in 2001.

Confronted with the obvious fact of rapidly declining child poverty in the late 1990s, opponents of welfare reform adopted a fallback position. They argued that reform had undermined the economic safety net. While reform might work well in good economic times, the weakened safety net would make the poor far more vulnerable to economic downturns. When a recession hit, children would be thrown into poverty in unusually large numbers.

Again, the exact opposite has occurred. Far from rising at above average rates, child poverty, for the first time, has remained flat during the recession.

Deep Child Poverty

Concern has been raised by some organizations concerning the so-called severity of child poverty. One measure of this concept is the percentage of children living in deep poverty, defined as children who live in families with annual incomes less than half the official poverty thresholds.

In 2001, 5.1 million children, or 7.1 percent of all children, lived in deep poverty. In contrast to child poverty in general, deep child poverty does appear to have increased slightly during 2001. However, the rate of deep child poverty in 2001 was lower than in 1995 prior to the enactment of reform, when the rate was 8.5 percent. There were some 800,000 fewer children living in deep poverty in 2001 than in 1995. The present deep child poverty rate is also lower than the rate at the beginning of the last recession in 1990, when the rate was 8.8 percent.

"In 2001, there were nearly 3 million fewer children in poverty than there had been before [welfare] reform."

Nonetheless, it is true that deep child poverty has declined less rapidly in the six years since welfare reform than has child poverty in single-mother families, or black and Hispanic child poverty, or child poverty in general. Welfare reform has clearly had less impact on this group than among the poor in general. Relatively few parents in these families are employed. The deep poverty group might best be viewed as the population that welfare reform has not yet reached. . . .

A Good Track Record

The record of welfare reform is striking. For a quarter-century prior to welfare reform, black child poverty and poverty among single mothers remained virtually frozen. After reform, poverty among both groups dropped rapidly, reaching the lowest levels in U.S. history. In all recessions since the beginning of the War on Poverty in the mid-1960s, child poverty has increased sharply; but in the recession of 2001, child poverty did not rise at all.

The track record of the past [several] years indicates that welfare reform should be strengthened and expanded. Regrettably, however, the numerous groups that adamantly opposed reform in 1996 have remained entrenched in their opposition. Despite occasional lip service to the contrary, these groups seek a de facto repeal of the current reform and enjoy strong support for their aims among liberals in the House and Senate.

The evidence demonstrates that, with welfare reform, our nation has found for the first time a successful policy that can lead to substantial long-term reductions in child poverty. Current efforts to undermine reform, if enacted, will have serious negative effects on the future well-being of low-income Americans.

The Difficulties of the Working Poor Are Overstated

by Larry Schweikart

About the author: *Larry Schweikart teaches history at the University of Dayton.*

When Barbara Ehrenreich's book *Nickel and Dimed: On (Not) Getting By in America* came out [in 2001] I knew it would be the perfect foil to another book I used in my classes, *The Millionaire Next Door*, by Thomas Stanley and William Danko (1996). Don't ever say that academics don't have a sense of humor.

At any rate, Ehrenreich must be given credit for at least entering the world of minimum-wage work, rather than sitting in her comfortable study or pontificating from a lofty perch at a think tank. The woman did get her hands dirty, quite literally. At times, a little less dirt and a little more scholarship might have been useful.

Ehrenreich conducted a live experiment in which she worked at minimum-wage jobs, living, as best she could, in whatever circumstances those wages would afford. She worked in Florida as a waitress at a greasy spoon, sometimes for $2.43 an hour, plus tips. Soon, she augmented her job with other work, such as housekeeping. Having satisfied herself with that part of her experiment, she moved on to Maine, where she toiled as a maid, and finally completed her research with a stint in Minnesota at Wal-Mart. She concluded that if she could have maintained her two-job regimen, and if she had no dire or sudden illnesses, she could have just barely gotten by. Despite her occasional genuinely funny quips—her exposition on feces, as a maid, is something to behold—her overall message is incredibly depressing and drenched in hopelessness. If her assessment is accurate, it is impossible to get by in America in low-level jobs. That's *if*.

A Flawed Analysis

Fortunately for many Americans—and for virtually all people who find themselves in these jobs—Ehrenreich's analysis has fatal flaws. Since it is certain this book will become the basis for many other "can't-get-by" studies that pass for policy analysis, it is worth analyzing her weaknesses in some detail.

First and foremost, Ehrenreich *pretended* to be a minimum-wage worker. She *acted* in a role for a few months. Critics might see this as supporting her position, but I think it blows up the entire foundation. The purpose of work is not to get by, but to get ahead. This is a critical distinction: how Ehrenreich looks at her work and life, and the reality of the situation. Most people, no matter what the job of the moment, see it as a way to get ahead later. Yet Ehrenreich did not even try to move up. She lied about her education and credentials at the outset so as to not prejudice the employers, either favorably (by giving her higher-paying positions) or negatively ("What's wrong with you that you can't find a gig with all your education?"). She apparently doesn't see this as a slap in the face for all those "proletarians" with whom she identifies who struggle to *get that GED*, or to get a college education at night.

Not only did she not try to advance, but she never sought out others who had. We learn about the private, sometimes tragic, lives of many of her co-workers, but never find anyone who made it into management, who left for greener pastures, or who even made it to the top of the low-level wage ladder. Quite the contrary, none of her managers are appealing: they are all greedy, petty, stupid, egotistical, and uncaring.

Since Ehrenreich's story involves personal experience as fact, my own background must be equally valid, if dated. When I turned 15, I got a minimum-wage job at Der Weinerschnitzel—the hotdog version of McDonald's. Almost instantly the manager (who was, as best I could tell, neither stupid or uncaring) was willing to make me an assistant manager. It had something to do with being able to remember to turn the sign off before I went home. Soon, I left the "dog house" for a better job, as a carryout boy at a local (and locally owned) grocery store. At the time I saw that as my big break: I started at $3.35 an hour, plus overtime, plus double time on holidays. Several women worked as cashiers there and had been there for years. Word got out that they earned more than $10 an hour! Again, while

> *"Most minimum-wage jobs are . . . entry-level [positions] designed to train people in basic skills."*

the managers did not baby us—they expected hard work and good habits, as well as a smile—we were well treated, and, for the day, well paid. It was an interracial staff, both among the carryout boys and the management. But no one there, unless someone was aiming at a managerial position, planned to stay at the grocery store his entire life. It was, as most minimum-wage jobs are, an entry-level position designed to train people in basic skills (working a cash register, counting change, stocking, taking inventory, ordering, and above all, being polite and energetic). . . .

Notable Absences

There was a flip side to Ehrenreich's self-imposed limits: "I had no intention of going hungry." Harsh as it may be, though, there is a powerful incentive when one goes hungry. It was exactly that kind of incentive, both in positive terms of advancing and in negative terms of utter failure, that rendered her experiment unrealistic.

If Ehrenreich missed this important (fundamental?) element to the world of minimum-wage work, or any work for that matter, what else did she miss? Plenty.

One is struck by the utter absence of marriage in this book. Most of Ehrenreich's sob-story examples are women who are single with children or are "living together." This is not a minor point. Charles Murray and others have demonstrated irrefutably that the single most important factor correlated with increasing wealth is marriage. Yet the author scarcely mentions marriage, as if it had no bearing on how some of her co-workers got where they were. One sees the subtle implications of this in her apparently unwitting choice of data from the Bureau of Labor Statistics which show that private household workers earn $23 a week less than the poverty level "for a family of three." A family of three is either a

> *"Most people, even poor people, have cars, televisions, VCRs, jewelry, or other items that constitute wealth."*

married couple with one child or a single-parent (usually a woman) with two kids. If the latter, this statistic almost by itself suggests that if there were two wage-earners, they would make well above the poverty level. In other words, the controlling factor is marriage, not wages.

Another thing is absent in the book: accumulated wealth. Everyone has something. Usually it's a house and "stuff," but most people, even poor people, have cars, televisions, VCRs, jewelry, or other items that constitute wealth. For Ehrenreich's experiment to "succeed" (for her to "not get by"), she had to *begin* with no wealth. She excludes a car from her equation and has no house, no tangibles, nothing to sell. Thus she began her experiment at a lower point than most of her subjects, many of whom at least owned cars and trailers (while Ehrenreich was renting transportation and living space at high weekly rates). Moreover, age is key to accumulating wealth: a 30-year-old has more stuff than a 20-year-old; a 50-year-old more than a 30-year-old; and so on. Part of "moving up" entails acquisition of things that you no longer have to purchase on a daily, or weekly, basis.

Ehrenreich's job choices, even within her narrow selections, were rigged to ensure the answer she wanted. She never took higher-paying jobs. Waiting tables can be low-paying, but it can also be quite lucrative. Waitresses at good restaurants and bars can pull in $100 a night, and in more upscale areas many times that. She might counter that she was too old or not good-looking enough for such gigs, but the elderly and, shall we say, "seasoned" ladies who occasionally wait on me at the pancake house or in some of the nicer restaurants are not Hollywood starlets. While it is true that Hooters has its own "look" when it comes to servers, most other establishments have no

> *"Waiting tables can be low-paying, but it can also be quite lucrative."*

problem hiring older men or women, as long as they are clean and dependable.

In some places, often when producing statistics that either are extremely controversial or barely believable ("30 percent of the workforce toils for $8 or less"), Ehrenreich relies on studies from predictably "liberal" think tanks. There is nothing wrong with that, if you also cite the other, conflicting evidence. How permanent are workers in this 30 percent? Not very, if most minimum-wage jobs are any indicator. Likewise, she claims that in "a survey conducted by the U.S. Conference of Mayors, 67 percent of the adults requesting emergency food aid are people with jobs." But her notes don't refer to any such study, only a *Detroit News* secondhand referral, which may, or may not, have gotten the details right. Again, though, the impression Ehrenreich gives is one of a massive subculture of minimum-wage peons, rather than the more accurate image of an escalator, in which some at the bottom rise all the way to the top, some get off on the second floor, and so on.

Where Are the Taxes?

While Ehrenreich spends many of her 200 pages detailing how she scrimped, cut corners, or otherwise tried to squeeze blood out of a Ding Dong, there is scarcely a word about taxes. The omission is staggering, especially considering her obsession, at times, with earning the additional 30 cents that one job offered over another. Consider this: Uncle Sam takes 10–25 percent of any worker's paycheck, right off the top, under "withholding." Gone. History. Vanished. In my state of Ohio, the government in Columbus takes another cut, around 6 percent. Dayton, where I work, and Springboro, where I live, also want their "take," slicing off yet another half a percent. And there is unemployment paid to the state—again, all coming right off the top. Then there is the Social Security and Medicare "contribution."

For middle-class employees these deductions are painful. But for low-income people they are nearly fatal. Most of Ehrenreich's co-workers would have had *double* the pay if not for the government's secular tithe. Maybe we can't get by without taxes, but let's assume, for a moment, that the federal tax rate was 15 percent. That would have saved most of Ehrenreich's colleagues up to 73 cents per hour (at $7.25). And how about if we assume that there is no state tax, as in

New Hampshire? That would add another 43 cents per hour. Social Security is a true luxury to people who need bigger paychecks now: would it not be wiser to let them keep their money at the front end? And unemployment? How many minimum-wage workers do you know who draw unemployment? Let's say that these "forced contributions" account for another 20 cents per hour. Merely by omitting these onerous taxes and other "contributions," we could give a hypothetical $7.25 per-hour employee a raise of up to $1.36, making the job $8.61. Spread over a 45-hour week (we'll assume a hard worker wants a little overtime), that could be an extra $61.20 *per week*, or an incredible $244.80 *per month*. This alone would have paid half the rent on a good apartment, not the sleazy motels that Ehrenreich had to frequent.

More taxes? Try this: the FICA "contribution" is paid half at the front end by the employee, but also half at the back end by the employee, even though the employer supposedly pays it. It is still the employee's money, but diverted from wages. Moreover, Ehrenreich disparages benefits and other "perks" as being preferred by employers because they are easier to take away in a crunch. She completely misses the obvious: to a point (I realize you cannot eat benefits), it is much more valuable to take a benefit than an extra dollar in salary. Consider health insurance. Employers can give an employee a dollar in benefits, a dollar that the employee could have used to purchase his own health care. But the benefit is pre-tax income; a dollar in benefits equals a dollar. After taxes, the dollar would be worth only about 65 cents to the employee.

There are even more tax issues that Ehrenreich carefully avoids when doing her survival assessments. If there is a tax incentive for home ownership, there is a corollary tax penalty for renting. There is a double tax penalty for renting motel rooms, which Ehrenreich had to rent until she could get an apartment, because most states tax them. What is troubling is that on multiple levels, and repeatedly, Ehrenreich refuses to even acknowledge, let alone consider, the impact of taxation on even the lowest-paid Americans because, apparently, it doesn't fit her mold.

Ehrenreich's proposals are predictable: a higher minimum wage, more welfare, more unionization. She admits that "nobody bothers to pull all these stories together" to proclaim a widespread state of emergency. That is precisely the point: these are disparate, isolated, and usually temporary stories, and when economists have "pulled them all together," they have not found anything near the minimum-wage hell to which Ehrenreich's denizens are damned. She wants to blame a "conspiracy of silence" for misrepresenting the "failure" of welfare reform, but the fact is that welfare reform, and minimum-wage work, have been studied extensively. Both the statistics, and the human success stories, reveal a different—and better—reality than the one Barbara Ehrenreich visited briefly in her search for "evidence."

Chapter 2

What Causes Poverty and Homelessness?

Chapter Preface

According to research conducted by the Domestic Policy Studies Department of the Heritage Foundation, children living with a single mother are six times more likely to live in poverty than are children whose parents are married. Moreover, 73 percent of the families earning the lowest wages are headed by single mothers, and at least 12.5 million children live in single-parent families that earn less than $15,000 a year. These children are more likely to drop out of school, take low-wage jobs, and become single parents themselves, perpetuating a cycle of intergenerational poverty, reports the Heritage Foundation.

The statistics on single parenthood and the poor have led many analysts to conclude that the absence of marriage in family life is a root cause of poverty. Arguing along similar lines, Harvard University fellow Lawrence Harrison maintains that cultural values and attitudes contribute significantly to poverty. In his opinion, "progress-prone" cultures, such as the mainstream Western culture, "share the belief that one's destiny can be influenced through considered action, and they attach high value to work, education, achieving, and saving." Conversely, "progress-resistant" cultures, including various third-world, immigrant, and rural American cultures, "tend to be passive and fatalistic, less entrepreneurial, less committed to education." Thus, Harrison concludes, if one is raised in a culture that de-emphasizes the importance of marriage and places a low priority on education and initiative, one is more likely to become resigned to poverty.

Other analysts, however, reject the theory that indigence is rooted in cultural attitudes and instead assert that poverty is the result of economic factors and systemic inequities. They point out, for example, that there has been a recent decline in lucrative work opportunities for low-skilled workers, mainly due to the loss of well-paying manufacturing jobs. Many of these employees have found work in the service industry, but these jobs pay less, are less stable, and offer few or no health care benefits. "Because of this," explains Aimee Molloy, a writer for the Center for Poverty Solutions, "we have seen an unprecedented incidence of chronic unemployment and underemployment." People working at the minimum wage typically do not earn a living wage—the income necessary for a family to meet its basic housing, food, health care, clothing, and transportation needs, Molloy points out. Workers who are unable to find jobs well above the minimum wage—or who do not have access to educational opportunities that would provide them with skills—fight a losing battle as they find themselves unable to afford housing, child care, or transportation to work. As Molloy states, "While the federal government has created programs to help poor families with child care expenses . . . only 10% of the families who qualify for federal child care [actually] receive assistance. Many cities have tens of thousands of people on waiting lists for child care programs." In addition, those poor workers who become homeless or who suffer from ill health face enormous barriers to keeping their jobs and working their way out of poverty. Such realities cannot be attributed to the cultural values of the poor, Molloy maintains.

While some experts assert that poverty stems from the absence of a two-parent family, inferior cultural values, or individual irresponsibility, others contend that long-standing socioeconomic inequities, stagnant wages, and inadequate public assistance programs are the main contributors to poverty. The authors in the following chapter continue this discussion in greater detail.

Broken Families and Single Parenthood Contribute to Poverty

by Patrick F. Fagan

About the author: *Patrick F. Fagan is William H.G. Fitzgerald Senior Fellow in Family and Cultural Issues at the Heritage Foundation, a public policy research institute that supports the ideas of limited government and the free market system.*

Much of the debate about the growing gap between rich and poor in America focuses on the changing job force, the cost of living, and the tax and regulatory structure that hamstrings businesses and employees. But analysis of the social science literature demonstrates that the root cause of poverty and income disparity is linked undeniably to the presence or absence of marriage. Broken families earn less and experience lower levels of educational achievement. Worse, they pass the prospect of meager incomes and family instability on to their children, ensuring a continuing if not expanding cycle of economic distress.

Simply put, whether or not a child's parents are married and stay married has a massive effect on his or her future prosperity and that of the next generation. Unfortunately, the growth in the number of children born into broken families in America—from 12 for every 100 born in 1950 to 58 for every 100 born in 1992—has become a seemingly unbreakable cycle that the federal government not only continues to ignore, but even promotes through some of its policies.

Numerous academic and social science researchers have demonstrated how the path to achieving a decent and stable income is still the traditional one: complete school, get a job, get married, then have children, in that order. Obviously, the journey toward a secure income can be derailed by choices growing children make, such as dropping out of school or getting pregnant before marriage. But generally, children who grow up in a stable, two-parent family have the best prospects for achieving income security as adults.

Because of recent advances in the methods social scientists and economists use to collect data, researchers are taking a broader intergenerational view of America's poor. From this vantage point, it has become clear that federal policies over the past three decades have promoted welfare dependency and single-parent families over married parents while frittering away the benefits of a vigorous free market and strong economy. Today, the economic and social future of children in the poor and the middle class is being undermined by a culture that promotes teenage sex, divorce, cohabitation, and out-of-wedlock birth.

Fortunately, the federal government and states and local communities can play important roles in changing this culture to ensure that all children reach their full income potential and do not languish in the poverty trap.

The Link Between Divorce and Poverty

To understand the importance of marriage to prosperity, and what the determinants of a stable marriage are, it is important to look first at the evidence surrounding the effects of its alternatives—divorce, cohabitation, and out-of-wedlock births—on children and on income.

Sadly, almost half of American families experience poverty following a divorce, and 75 percent of all women who apply for welfare benefits do so because of a disrupted marriage or a disrupted relationship in which they live with a male outside of marriage.

Divorce has many harmful effects on the income of families and future generations. Its immediate effects can be seen in data reported in 1994 by Mary Corcoran, a professor of political science at the University of Michigan: "During the years children lived with two parents, their family incomes averaged $43,600, and when these same children lived with one parent, their family incomes averaged $25,300." In other words, the household income of a child's family dropped on average about 42 percent following divorce. By 1997, 8.15 million children were living with a divorced single parent. . . .

As substantial as this income reduction is, little public attention is paid to the relationship between the breakdown of marriage and poverty. Consider, by comparison, the reaction to a comparable decrease in the national economy. When America's economic productivity fell by 2.1 percent from 1981 to 1982, it was called a recession. And when the economy contracted by 30.5 percent from $203 million to $141 million (in constant 1958 dollars) from 1929 to 1933, it was called the Great Depression. Yet each and every year for the past [three decades] over one

> *"The root cause of poverty and income disparity is linked undeniably to the presence or absence of marriage."*

million children have experienced divorce in their families with an associated reduction in family income that ranged from 28 percent to 42 percent. It is no wonder that three-fourths of all women applying for welfare benefits do so because of a disruption of marriage.

Understandably, mothers who are employed at the time of divorce are much less likely to become welfare recipients than are mothers who do not work. And mothers who are not employed in the workforce at the time of divorce are as close to going on welfare as are single mothers who lose their jobs. Divorce is the main factor in determining the length of "poverty spells," particularly for women whose pre-divorce family income was in the bottom half of the income distribution. Divorce, then, poses the greatest threat to women in low-income families. Moreover, almost 50 percent of households with children move into poverty following divorce. Simply put, divorce has become too prevalent and affects an ever-increasing number of children.

In the 1950s, the rate of divorce was lower among high-income groups; by 1960, there was a convergence of rates among all socioeconomic groups. By 1975, for the first time, more marriages ended in divorce than in death. Since 1960, there has been a significant shift in the ratio of children deprived of married parents by death compared with those so deprived by divorce. Compared with the number of children who lost a parent through death, 75 percent, 150 percent, and 580 percent as many, respectively, lost a parent through divorce in 1960, in 1986, and in 1995.

Divorce is linked to a number of serious problems beyond the immediate economic problem of lost income. For instance, the children of divorced parents are more likely to get pregnant and give birth outside of marriage, especially if the divorce occurred during their mid-teenage

> *"Almost half of American families experience poverty following a divorce."*

years, and twice as likely to cohabit than are children of married parents. Moreover, divorce appears to result in a reduction of the educational accomplishments of the affected children, weakens their psychological and physical health, and predisposes them to rapid initiation of sexual relationships and higher levels of marital instability. It also raises the probability that they will never marry, especially for boys.

For a mother with children, divorce increases her financial responsibility and, typically, her hours of labor outside the home. Divorce and additional work hours also disrupt her network of support for parenting her children. These additional stresses take their toll: Single mothers experience increased levels of physical and mental illness, addictions, and even suicide following divorce. All of these outcomes have an effect on family income.

Moreover, the consequences of divorce flow from generation to generation, since the children of divorce are more likely to experience the same problems and pass them on to their own children. Significantly, these effects are markedly different from the effect that the death of a married parent has on children; in fact, such children are *less* likely than the average to divorce when they grow up.

Divorce and Assets

Little research has been done on the effect of divorce on the assets accumulated over time by a household, but a RAND Corporation study indicates that the effect may be dramatic: Family structure is strongly tied to wealth by the time one reaches the sixth decade of life. The assets of married couples in their fifties (who are approaching retirement) are four times greater than those of their divorced peers. Even when the two divorced households' assets on average are combined, the RAND study shows that their asset base is half that of married couples.

"Three-fourths of all women applying for welfare benefits do so because of a disruption of marriage."

Upon reflection, this makes sense. After a divorce, the largest asset—the family home—frequently is sold and the proceeds used to finance the divorce and start new homes. In addition, the evidence indicates that the income of divorced households with children drops significantly, thereby lessening the likelihood of asset formation.

Cohabitation and Divorce

Our understanding of cohabitation's effect on income derives, to date, mainly from its significant relationship to divorce. People who live together before marrying divorce at about twice the rate of couples who do not cohabit before marriage, and four times the rate if they marry someone other than their present partner. Furthermore, many of these young adults express uncertainty about their future together. It is both a direct and an indirect factor in reducing average family income.

Today, more Americans than ever before are living together before marriage—an average of 1.5 years. Men and women in their twenties and thirties are living together at much the same rate as before, but with a significant difference: Many more now cohabit rather than marry.

The proportion of marriages preceded by a period of cohabitation increased from 8 percent in the late 1960s to 49 percent in 1985. Over half of Americans in their thirties today live in a cohabiting relationship, and more than half of recent marriages were preceded by cohabitation. Larry Bumpass, a University of Wisconsin–Madison professor in the Center for Demography and Ecology, noted in an address to the Population Association of America that "Sex, living arrangements and parenting depend less on marriage."

One reason for this change in American values lies with parents who divorce: Their children are more likely to cohabit before marriage as young adults. In 1990, 29 percent of those who had continually married parents had cohabited before their own marriage, but between 54 percent and 62 percent of children from divorced families cohabited before marriage.

Cohabitation doubles the rate of divorce, and the rates double again for those who cohabit before marriage with someone other than a future spouse. Forty percent of cohabiting couples have children in the home, and 12 percent of all cohabiting couples have had a biological child during cohabitation. More than half of adults (56 percent) who live together outside of marriage and beget children and then marry will divorce. About 80 percent of children who have lived in a household with cohabiting parents will spend some of their childhood in a single-parent home.

Given this high level of disruption, cohabitation can be a good marker of future weakness in household income and the economic and social situation of children in these unions. The problem is further aggravated by the growing cultural acceptance of what used to be described as "illicit" relationships. Larry Bumpass found that by the early 1990s, only 20 percent of young adults disapproved of premarital sex, even for 18-year-olds, and that only one-sixth explicitly disapproved of cohabitation under any circumstances.

Out-of-Wedlock Births and Poverty

Today, social science research broadly characterizes the children who are most likely to attain a good income as adults: They have parents who are married; they finish school, get a job, abstain from intercourse until marriage, and marry before having children of their own. But family structure plays an even larger role in children's future prosperity than those who have formulated public policy over the past 30 years have been willing to admit.

Having a baby out of wedlock usually derails progress toward achieving a stable family structure and income. Teenage out-of-wedlock births rose from 15 percent of all teen births in 1960 to 76 percent in 1994. Fewer than one-third of those who have a baby before reaching age 18 complete high school, compared with the 50 percent completion rate for teens of similar backgrounds who avoid pregnancy.

It is not that the number of babies born to teens has changed; it is that marriage within this group has vanished. In addition, almost half of the mothers of out-of-wedlock children will go on to have another child out of wedlock.

The vast majority of out-of-wedlock births occur to mature adults age 20 and older, and more out-of-wedlock births occur to women over 30 than to teens below age 18; the number is eight times higher for second out-of-wedlock births. The increase in these births among older women accompanies a decline in teenage out-of-wedlock births and abortions.

> *"Cohabitation can be a good marker of future weakness in household income."*

Two very different changes in American society may explain this decline: the rise in teenage virginity and an increase in the use of contraceptives. The editor of *Teen People* magazine recently reported very high interest among teenagers in the subject of virginity. Access to the specific implant contraceptives Depro-

Provera and Norplant also has been associated (but not documented as yet) with the reduction in the number of out-of-wedlock teen births. Aside from the avoidance of pregnancy, the decision not to abstain from sex is linked to habits of risk-taking related to alcohol and drug abuse, school dropout rates, and crime.

More than any other group, teenage mothers who give birth outside of marriage spend more of their lives as single parents. Not surprisingly, their children spend more time in poverty than do the children of any other family structure.

A single-parent family background and the poverty that usually accompanies it render children twice as likely to drop out of high school, 2.5 times as likely to become out-of-wedlock teen parents, and 1.4 times as likely to be unemployed. These teens miss more days of school, have lower educational aspirations, receive lower grades, and eventually divorce more often as adults. They are almost twice as likely to exhibit antisocial behavior as adults; 25 percent to 50 percent more likely to manifest such behavioral problems as anxiety, depression, hyperactivity, or dependence; two to three times more likely to need psychiatric care; and much more likely to commit suicide as teenagers.

Mark Testa, a professor in the University of Chicago's School of Social Service Administration, conducted studies that show the linkage between family background, education, and work habits and out-of-wedlock pregnancy. According to Testa, "premarital pregnancy risks are significantly higher among single women

> *"Children [of teen mothers] spend more time in poverty than do the children of any other family structure."*

who are not in school or [are] out of work and who have dropped out of high school. Being raised in a family that received welfare also appears to raise the risk of premarital pregnancy."

The research of Yuko Matsuhashi of the University of California at San Diego and his colleagues shows that few mothers (14 percent) were living with both parents at the time of their first out-of-wedlock baby's conception, and fewer still (2 percent) were living with both parents at the time of their second baby's conception. In other words, single-parent households become much more entrenched with the second baby, and fewer of these mothers stay in school, thereby lessening their chances of attaining a good income in the future.

Nearly 80 percent of men do not marry the teenage mothers of their children. Nonetheless, cohabitation and cooperation in some form generally does occur between biological parents. About 40 percent of mothers plan to care for their first baby with the father of the baby, but not to marry him. Many more mothers of second out-of-wedlock babies plan to take care of their babies alone than do the mothers of first out-of-wedlock babies, and fewer of them live with their own parents. The downward economic spiral accelerates.

Typically, the household income of those who have out-of-wedlock children in their teens is low. Over 75 percent will be on welfare within five years. These women comprise more than half of all mothers on welfare. The average family income for children who lived with their never-married mothers was only about 40 percent of the family income for children who lived with either a divorced or a widowed mother. The family background of most teenage out-of-wedlock mothers includes such factors as early age at marriage (or cohabitation) for the teen mother's own parents and lower educational levels for both the teen mother's parents and the teen mother herself.

The Family Structure of Child Poverty

As Chart 1 shows, the relationship between poverty and the absence of intact marriages is indeed very strong. The continuous cooperation and lifelong commitment involved in marriage have much to do with significant income differences in households with children. For example:

• *The vast majority of children who live with a single parent are in households in the bottom 20 percent of earnings.* Specifically, about 74 percent of families with children in the lowest income quintile are headed by single par-

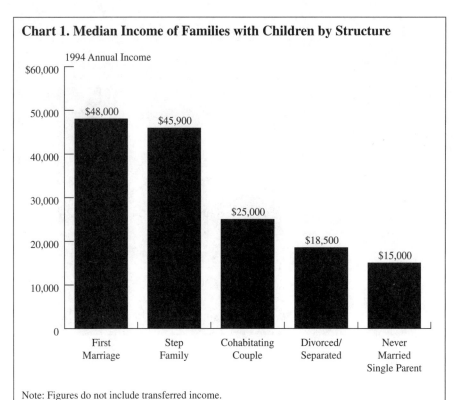

Chart 1. Median Income of Families with Children by Structure

1994 Annual Income

First Marriage: $48,000
Step Family: $45,900
Cohabitating Couple: $25,000
Divorced/Separated: $18,500
Never Married Single Parent: $15,000

Note: Figures do not include transferred income.
Source: Heritage Center for Data Analysis calculations based on data from *1995 Survey of Consumer Finance*, Federal Reserve Board.

ents. Conversely, 95 percent of families with children in the highest quintile of income are headed by married parents.

• *Children living with a single mother are six times more likely to live in poverty than are children whose parents are married.* (See Chart 2) As this analysis will show, family background also can be linked with less education and fewer hours worked, on average, when the child grows up.

• *Over 12.5 million children in 1994 lived in single-parent families that earned less than $15,000 per year.* Only 3 million such children lived with families that had annual incomes greater than $30,000. . . .

Marriage, Education, and Income

The research discussed above clearly indicates that family structure has much to do with income levels and asset building, both of which lead to economic prosperity. This section will explain why this occurs.

A family's income is used to finance immediate needs and, if it is sufficient, may allow the family to save for future needs. There are two elements in the amount of income received: the dollar value of hours worked and the number of

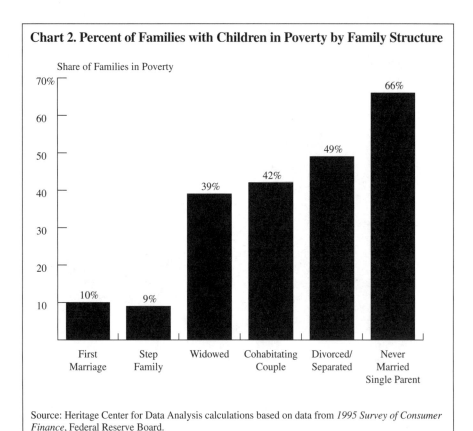

Chart 2. Percent of Families with Children in Poverty by Family Structure

Share of Families in Poverty

First Marriage: 10%
Step Family: 9%
Widowed: 39%
Cohabitating Couple: 42%
Divorced/Separated: 49%
Never Married Single Parent: 66%

Source: Heritage Center for Data Analysis calculations based on data from *1995 Survey of Consumer Finance*, Federal Reserve Board.

hours worked. These in turn are affected by, among other things, the parents' education level and work habits that typically are formed in the early years.

The marriage of the parents has much to do with a child's educational attainment and work ethic. The relationship can be expressed as an equation: Income = (education attained) × (work ethic) × (unity of family structure). . . .

Of course, one does not obtain an adequate and steady income just by marrying. Increasing the number of hours worked at a job valued by the marketplace will provide more income. The number of hours worked is linked directly to educational achievement and family structure. Families whose members have lower levels of education normally will have to work longer to reach a modest level of financial security than do those whose members achieve higher levels of education.

However, people who are not married and have less education work the fewest hours per year. In general, married couples have higher levels of education and work longer and make sure that their children achieve higher levels of education.

Although the income of a family household depends on the educational level of parents, it is the parents' *income* rather than their *level of education* that predicts more accurately the level of education their children will achieve. In general, children with high-income parents receive more education than do children of lower-income parents. But higher income is less likely without marriage (see Chart 1), and poverty is much more likely without it.

"The relationship between poverty and the absence of intact marriages is indeed very strong."

Education gives the child from a high-income family a great advantage. The federal government's Panel Study of Income Dynamics showed the large economic gains that can be realized by completing high school, both in the level of wages earned and in the longer hours per week that a person will work. But family background accounts for at least half the variance in educational attainment. Students from intact families score more positively on all measures than do those from both step and single-parent families. Adolescents who do not live with both natural parents are at significantly greater risk of leaving high school before graduating. And the number of years of education received translates into a better first job and better jobs later at higher salaries.

Marriage, Work Ethic, and Income

A significant portion of two-parent families have moved out of the poverty range because both parents work, which also increases—and in many cases doubles—the total number of hours worked within the household. Among America's poor, there has been a significant shift in the number of hours worked per household, which indicates that much of the disparity in young men's economic status is concentrated in the number of hours worked.

In 1960, nearly two-thirds of households in the bottom quintile of income were headed by individuals who worked—primarily married fathers. By 1991, this figure had fallen to around one-third, and only 11 percent of these households were headed by someone who worked full-time throughout the year.

The total number of hours worked in married households has increased significantly over the past 40 years. According to former Congressional Budget Office Director June O'Neill, in 1950 only 18 percent of married mothers with children under 18 worked outside the home. By 1975, 41 percent of married mothers worked and that proportion reached 64 percent in 1992. Yet mothers on welfare appear to work little—only 7 percent report any employment.[1]

Not only are those in the lowest quintile generally working fewer hours than their counterparts were in the 1950s and 1960s, but they are doing so despite a national family trend in the rising number of hours worked.

A reverse trend accompanies the disappearance of marriage: The number of hours worked in the family household declines. Present-day single heads of households are working fewer hours than the married heads of poor households in the 1950s (typically, married men). At the same time, married couples are increasing the total number of hours worked, and although there are some unwelcome consequences from this increase in working hours in married households, there is no doubt that it has increased the number of families exiting a life of poverty.

---

1. These data were collected before the enforcement of the 1996 Welfare Reform Act.

Single Mothers Are Unfairly Blamed for Poverty

by Lori Holyfield

About the author: *Lori Holyfield is the author* of Moving Up and Out: Poverty, Education, and the Single Parent Family.

Ideologically, it seems that it is not so important to us, as Americans, that we all be equal, as it is that we all have equal opportunities. These views often boil down to individual theories of shame and blame. If the world in fact worked as we would like to believe, Americans could count on rewards matching investment. In other words, the harder we work, and the more perseverance and ambition we demonstrate, the greater will be our reward. When we achieve success, we give ourselves the credit. When we fail, we blame ourselves. This thinking appeals to us because it seems neither complicated nor unfair; poor people are poor simply because they are not trying as hard as the rest of us. Popular notions reflect these images. After all, we all know someone who applied himself or herself and "made" it.

Opinion polls bear this out. For example, in 1990 the National Opinion Research Center (NORC) found that 40 percent of Americans believed too much was being spent on welfare. By 1994, that number had risen to 65 percent. The AFDC [Aid to Families with Dependent Children] program was strongly criticized for costing too much, even though it accounted for only about 1 percent of the federal budget. In other words, combined expenditures for AFDC, food stamps, and Medicaid total approximately $117 billion per year. On the other hand, "wealth-fare" or "aid to dependent corporations" cost taxpayers an estimated $730 billion over a five-year period from 1995 to 2000. Broken down, that means $146 billion in aid to the rich versus $117 billion for a combination of services to the poor. Moreover, in the mid-1990s, Citizens for Tax Justice reported that corporations were enjoying tax breaks that equaled an estimated

$200 billion and that a few hundred large corporations were benefiting from the bulk of the savings. Property and estate tax deductions, charitable contributions, and mortgage interest deductions all serve to benefit those in the upper-middle and upper classes disproportionately. Current tax reform by the Bush administration has been criticized for benefiting only the wealthiest families in the United States. In other words, tax loopholes for the very rich and corporations are entitlement programs that remain largely invisible to American taxpayers.

The "Welfare Mother" Myth

Another myth, which I find difficult to dispel in my sociology classes, is that welfare mothers get into the welfare system and stay there. In fact, according to some studies, two-thirds of those who received AFDC benefits exited the programs within two years. Only 9 percent stayed for more than seven years, and less than 10 percent stayed more than eight years. Until the 1996 welfare reform, those most likely to have lengthy stays on welfare were young single mothers with children under the age of three.

Single mothers are especially sensitive to this myth. In an earlier research project, I learned that welfare-to-work participants wanted others to know that their tenure on public assistance was short. This belief that assistance should be as brief as possible resonated with me because I remember having set a deadline for myself. I wanted to be able to say that I had received food stamps for less than a year. That somehow made it seem more temporary. The longer I needed assistance, the more I came to identify myself as a welfare recipient, an identity I very much wanted to avoid.

The myth that welfare mothers have too many children is equally popular. Arkansas politicians were so concerned about this issue that they enacted a measure referred to as the "family cap." It denies additional money to women if they have children while on welfare. The first problem with this myth is that 84 percent of TANF [Temporary Assistance to Needy Families] single parents have just one or two children, the average for the general population. Second, the notion that welfare is too generous and that women have children in order to increase their welfare payments, frankly, makes no sense. Allowances for additional births range from $27 to $147 per child, depending upon the state of residence, figures that do not begin to match the expense of an additional child.

> *"[One] persistent myth is that the children of welfare mothers will become welfare users themselves."*

Another persistent myth is that the children of welfare mothers will become welfare users themselves. Deena, a social worker with a twenty-year-old son, explained to me how she worried about being on welfare because she wanted her son to have a strong work ethic. "I was particularly concerned with that," she explained, "because I had public assistance, and I didn't want him to be a second generation on public assistance."

For the small proportion of children who later go on welfare themselves, situational factors such as employment difficulties, spousal non-support, and transportation problems may better explain continued use than the more popular perceptions of moral corruption or laziness. I have always been perplexed by the sarcasm attached to public discussions of intergenerational poverty. Perhaps the rhetoric surrounding this particular myth is so harsh because children are at the center of the debate. Comments made by legislators while hashing out the 1988 Family Support Act, which became law under President [Ronald] Reagan, reflect this attitude: "This legislation is designed to reach those children of welfare mothers who grow up learning more about the welfare office than an employment office. . . . A reform with mandatory participation will break the welfare dependency cycle in those families who prefer a welfare check to a paycheck."

This kind of thinking is in many ways flawed. Even poor families not on welfare struggle to provide a safe, nurturing environment for their children. Research shows that when education and routine structure (a near impossibility for poor single parents) and access to regular health care are present, children fare much better, even in poorest families. Despite that in Arkansas the proportion of children living in poverty went from 27.4 percent in 1979 to 16.3 percent in 1998, programs are still needed to serve children entering school, who require health care, child care services, and nutritional support.

> *"Popular sentiment creates a double stigma for women who are both black and poor."*

Indeed, some research has found that children in families receiving welfare are at least able to obtain somewhat routine medical and dental care. If it is the children for whom we are concerned, state programs must build upon this knowledge and provide permanent change via education and create real potential for living wages.

More Myths About the Poor

Even more myths abound. For example, there is the notion that most welfare recipients are African American teenage mothers who live in inner cities. In fact, most welfare recipients are white, although the proportion who are African American is higher than their representation in the general population since they are much poorer as a group.

Louise, an African American single mother and former scholarship recipient who was once on welfare, is now working toward her master's degree in education. She remains excruciatingly aware of the welfare stigma. Although it has been two years since Louise received any assistance, she explains, "I'm really still embarrassed about it. I know what people say, but I didn't have a choice." Many women shared Louise's insight, realizing that popular sentiment creates a double stigma for women who are both black and poor.

Another popular myth depicts welfare recipients as lazy. Yet in 1994, 18 percent of full-time incomes remained below the poverty level and 50 percent of all families in poverty were headed by someone who worked. One-third of those worked full-time jobs. Moreover, AFDC had such strict limits that many women feared losing their benefits if they earned money in addition to their monthly stipends. Their fears were not unfounded. Julie, a mother of two, remembers, "If I earned any cash I kept my mouth shut, and there was always a sense of anxiety or, I guess, guilt. You couldn't be just poor. You had to be dirt poor."

> *"Even though many welfare recipients work at least part time, they are seen as lacking in initiative."*

Martha was one of those who worked full-time but remained poor. She has three children, two grown and one still at home. Martha remembers when she was earning too much to qualify for food stamps. "When I worked for the health department," she explained, "I made too much to get food stamps because I made about eight hundred dollars a month and by it being just the two of us, I could have gotten eight or nine dollars [in food stamps] a month, but it wasn't worth all the paperwork and all of the time I had to spend down there [at the social services office]."

As most Americans understand, $800 per month is hardly enough to cover housing and utility costs, much less clothing, child care, transportation, health care, and other living expenses. But the system used to measure poverty has changed little since it was established during the Johnson administration, nearly 40 years ago. Today, the Census Bureau provides statistics on those within 125 percent of the official poverty level, a far more realistic measurement given the numerous increases in non-food costs. When we add this group, the number of those in poverty is close to 18 percent.

Why are these false and damaging stereotypes so enduring? As I talked with women throughout the state of Arkansas, I wondered if perhaps it has to do with our own fears. Perhaps it is too frightening to acknowledge that even though some people are trying their best, they still slip through the safety net. It simply does not fit the American dream. It seems that we hold strongly to the egalitarian ethos that we all have the same ability and opportunity for upward mobility, but when success eludes us, for whatever reason, the blame game begins.

Internalized Blame

What surprised me most during my research was the degree to which so many of the women shared these images of themselves. In retrospect, I should have anticipated this. After all, the negative messages about welfare carry with them a surge of moral legitimation from the media to politicians to even the clergy. By this, I mean that the popular images brought forth are jam-packed with justifications that are largely taken for granted. For example, even though many welfare recipients work at least part time, they are seen as lacking in initiative. Opinion polls reveal that "lack of effort" is the typical explanation for welfare dependence. Yet most of these women worked at full-time jobs before they returned to school, and each of them made at or near poverty wages. Like more than 13 million other Americans, they were trapped in the "low-wage twilight zone."

Resisting the cultural scripts and the inclination to blame oneself is difficult. "I think it comes from inside you," says Madonna, a mother of five. "I just know the things I heard from my family. I know the rhetoric I hear on television about generations of recipients, yada yada." But even though Madonna worked full-time, she still qualified for food stamps to feed her family. "If I just got paid better," she continued. "Why is my life not worth as much as someone who does something that I don't do? It's not exactly my fault. What is my fault, if you can call it a fault, is that I've got five children." Madonna's ambivalence was reflected time and time again by others who faced the same dilemmas.

While the women were susceptible to the popular notions, they seemed to be able to separate themselves from them, referring more often to "circumstances" than "lack of effort." The effect was what sociologists describe as role distancing—attempting to ensure that they were not confused with a "typical" welfare recipient. Martha, for example, considered herself very different from the stereotype:

> Certain single parents survive by being single parents. There are some that say, "Well, I can get this and the government will take care of us. And they'll give us food stamps and we can get a house to move into." And that's how they survive by not wanting to work. And that's the ones that give us a bad name.

Martha did not know that other single mothers, like herself, were struggling with full-time jobs. She just knew that she was doing it "by the book" and, just as Madonna found, it was not enough.

"'You definitely feel people . . . staring at you when you're paying for things with food stamps.'"

Sarah was especially quick to distance herself from the stereotype. As she put it, she was not so concerned for herself as she was for "typical" single mothers:

> I had a brain. I always had options. Somehow, I've always managed to keep a roof over our head and a decent car to drive. But think of all the women who have no cars to drive and no sense, and may be a little retarded or something. Those children, I mean, what are those children going to grow up with? They don't even know how to feed them.

Many of the women in the study saw themselves as atypical. At first I worried that this attitude might give them a distorted view of themselves and their circumstances. But over time I began to understand their attempts to distance themselves from others. They had become warriors in a battle to survive the barrage of stigmatizing rhetoric. This was their only defense. Karen Seccombe deals extensively with this subject in her study of welfare recipients' perceptions of welfare. She writes:

> Social arrangements, which are in the best interest of the dominant group, are presented as being in everyone's best interests. Subordinates come to accept these interests as their own, and the contradictions inherent in the interests of the dominant and subordinate groups are ignored. Thus, the ideology becomes "common sense" and normative, and cohesion is created where there would otherwise be conflict. The ideologies reflect the interests and perspectives of the elite, but the poor, who fail to see the shared political nature of their problems, also internalize them.

Poverty, a social phenomenon, becomes relegated to the realm of personal problems.

Stigma and Labels

The moral overtones become heavy and difficult to battle as critics argue that by eliminating welfare and government aid to single parents, we can better help them to achieve self-sufficiency. Unless a person has experienced the deep isolation of poverty, and the diminished self-esteem it brings, it is difficult to appreciate the power of such punitive rhetoric.

"We see those who are struggling as somehow deficient while those who 'make it' are held in great esteem."

Laura shared the same ambivalence about asking for public assistance, but knew she had to provide for her two sons. "I felt like pond scum," she remembered, "but that didn't deter me from asking." Indeed, each of the women felt the social stigma in very personal ways. Laura's comment resonated with me personally. I, too, remember feeling my self-worth plummet in settings where I felt guilty for having to receive assistance. It was only after I began to study sociology that I realized the power that being labeled a "welfare mother" had over me.

Social labels are important. Particular kinds can have negative influence and seriously alter our self-concepts when our identities are discredited. Moreover, attacks on our selves are especially destructive when we are powerless to combat them.

Interestingly, for these women the most memorable examples of humiliation took place in a public setting most of us would consider neutral territory—the grocery store. A trip to the grocery store with what Sonya's child called "funny money" transforms the store into a public setting for rituals of self-degradation, in part because the stigma becomes visible the moment one presents food stamps at the check-out counter. "You definitely feel people giving you dirty looks and staring at you when you're paying for things with food stamps," Rene recalls. She learned to avoid certain cashiers and remembers once having to go to the post office to pick up her food stamp allotment. "Every so often they would send it certified mail, I guess just to make sure the right person was getting it. The guy working behind the counter [was] being real friendly until he came back with what he knew was food stamps . . . and being very cold when he handed them to me. There's definitely stigma attached.". . .

Punitive Rhetoric

The stigma felt by these women is part of the morality trap that many Americans fall into when they become financially dependent upon the government. But as some critics point out, we often forget that the system of welfare and the phenomenon of single parenting are hardly gender-neutral. To state, as one Congressman did, "If there's a minimum wage job out there, we expect you to take it," is to ignore the real needs and concerns of poverty and instead to adopt a punitive, moralistic stance that fails to recognize the difficulties that working mothers face with respect to child care, health care, child support, and the workplace. Karen Seccombe writes: "[T]hese discussions [of welfare reform] are problematic because they assume that welfare is a gender neutral program. It is not. Recipients are predominantly women, and the needs and concerns embedded in women's real life experiences as caretakers of children are not contextualized within their recommendations to reduce or eliminate welfare."

Maintaining a consistent self-image over time requires social support. And because our culture values ambition and hard work, we see those who are struggling as somehow deficient while those who "make it" are held in great esteem. We hold tightly to the "rags to riches" stories in our culture, however rare they may be. Wealthy people are assumed to have succeeded because they simply tried harder than everyone else; thus they must possess a stronger work ethic. We have our American heroes: the Horatio Alger types like Sam Walton or Bill Gates. They are believed to be more willing to take risks and possess drives that are unique to hard-working individuals. If you are a successful person, you are also likely to develop feelings of self-efficacy, that is, a belief that your own actions bring rewards. The process is circular: those with higher rewards elicit more respect from others, which in turn legitimates their status and makes it easier to reject negative social labels and manage the impressions of others.

> *"Poverty is more than an individual problem."*

Finally, there is the good old-fashioned "luck of the draw," otherwise known as fatalism. This equally simplistic view has always been one of my favorites. After all, who among us has not had visions of waking up to find the Publisher's Clearinghouse van parked in our driveway, or buying that one lucky lottery ticket? Believing in luck implies that much of what happens to us is really fate. We are poor or wealthy because of luck. Our relative positions in life are nothing more than "quirks of birth, human nature, chance and related forces," each beyond our control.

Growing up in the same small town as Sam Walton, I have seen first-hand that being in the right place at the right time can bring a huge payoff. When I was a child, my mother often said, "Everything that happens to us has a purpose. Things don't happen without a reason." But it was also my mother who told me, "Part of life is what happens, and the rest is how you deal with it." Taken separately, her comments have contradictory meanings; but taken together, they hold great wisdom. Being born poor is indeed a condition of fate. Remaining poor may be better understood through what sociologists describe as "structural" explanations.

More than an Individual Problem

Using a sociological framework, we are forced to acknowledge that poverty is more than an individual problem. Rather, there are patterns to this phenomenon. We find that welfare dependency is hardly gender-neutral, inasmuch as women and children largely constitute the poor. The fact that some segments of society are more likely to be poor than others begs an investigation of the economic and social factors that disadvantage entire groups.

I have found in my college teaching experience that to talk about children in poverty is one thing, but I need only mention the terms "welfare" and "discrimination" and most students tune out. This holds even though most "welfare" recipients are children. Perhaps the resistance is due to the fact that in today's race- and class-segregated world, the middle class and wealthy do not ordinarily interact with the poor, while the working class cannot afford to. First, they are too busy trying to keep themselves out of poverty. Second, if they examine poverty too closely, it might reveal the false hopes to which many in the working class necessarily cling. Their own springboards to higher-paying jobs may not be broken, but they are seriously cracked. When we consider the distribution of household incomes among Americans, we see that a small proportion earns most of the income (see Table 1).

As Table 1 reveals, while the median annual income for the wealthiest fifth of the American populace was $127,529 in 1998, the poorest fifth had to get by on $9,223. The stock market boom of the 1990s failed to benefit many hard-working American citizens 34 million of whom can be officially classified as poor. The current official system for measuring poverty has been challenged on a number of

> *"Interventions . . . must come in the form of opportunities that can actually reduce the incidence of poverty."*

points. Critics argue that a more realistic measure would significantly raise the number of those counted as poor.

In 1995 the National Academy of Sciences published a report from a panel that had studied the official poverty measures that have been in place since 1969. Among the recommendations to emerge from the study were that the

Table 1. Mean Household Income and Share of Aggregate Income by Quintile, 1998

Quintile	Mean Household Income (dollars)	Share of Aggregate Household Income (percentage)
Lowest fifth	9,223	3.6
Second fifth	23,288	9.0
Third fifth	38,967	15.0
Fourth fifth	60,266	23.2
Highest fifth	127,529	49.2

Source: Mean household income figures from U.S. Bureau of the Census, 1998, "Money Income of Households, Families, and Persons in the United States: 1998." *Current Population Reports*, Series P-60. Washington, DC: U.S. Government Printing Office. Share of aggregate income from U.S. Bureau of the Census, 1998. "Household Wealth and Asset Ownership: 1998." *Current Population Reports*, Series P-70. Washington, DC: U.S. Government Printing Office.

poverty threshold should be adjusted to better represent the costs of food, clothing, shelter (including utilities), everyday needs, child-care costs, medical out-of-pocket expenses, work-related costs, and cost-of-living variations based on geographic location. The study also recommended that the measure should count the value of in-kind benefits, such as food stamps, subsidized housing, school lunches, and home energy assistance. The federal Office of Management and Budget encouraged the Bureau of the Census to provide experimental poverty figures to reflect these recommendations. Using these measures, the rate of poverty is, not surprisingly, significantly higher—as high as 18 percent, as mentioned earlier.

A Social Issue

Finally, as sociologist C. Wright Mills argued, when a social phenomenon affects significant segments of a population, it is no longer a personal trouble but instead becomes a social issue. Let us consider, then, the phenomenon of poor children, the most vulnerable of the poor. Statistics reveal that poor children tend to have lower academic achievement than other children. It is true that they are more likely to drop out of school, become parents in adolescence, and be jobless. And they are more likely to suffer health problems, including low birth weight, malnutrition, sudden infant death, and birth defects. Poor children are more likely to be victims of homicide and suicide. They are more likely to be neglected and to suffer serious injury from abuse. Children of the poor are more likely to experience social withdrawal, depression, and low self-esteem, and to suffer from various behavioral disorders.

Interventions are needed to help reduce the "cycle of poverty," but these must come in the form of opportunities that can actually reduce the incidence of poverty. Punitive measures do not move people out of poverty. If anything, they disarm poor people, making them less able to cope with an already enormous task of survival. At best, the welfare reform measures currently in place transform the poor into the "working poor" but seldom reduce the odds against them. What researchers agree on, however, is that there is continued promise when education is a key ingredient. But first it has to be accessible.

Personal Irresponsibility Causes Poverty

by Blake Hurst

About the author: *Blake Hurst is a Missouri farmer.*

"Diana" age 20, showed up [in the spring of 1999] at our wholesale green-house here in northwest Missouri in search of a job. Cheryl, a former employee of ours, accompanied her. Diana had a hard luck story, was recommended by Cheryl, and was down to her last cent: so my wife Julie hired her.

She showed up for work for three days, missed a day, then needed her check on Saturday, one week earlier than normal. Julie told her to come and work on Saturday, and we would figure her paycheck at the end of the day. Saturday, she called up and couldn't come to work because she had had a headache on Friday. Monday, she was absent again, presumably still recovering from Friday's head-ache, but did send Cheryl to pick up her check. Tuesday, she missed work again. Ditto Wednesday. On Thursday, she finally put in an appearance. She had the misfortune to come into the office when Julie and I were both there, and had to undergo a tag-team attitude adjustment session. At noon, she left for good. We had made it clear that we would give her another chance, but she de-clined the offer.

People Do Not Help Themselves

You can't help but have sympathy for someone living in poverty. But my sympathy is tempered by the two or three phone calls I receive every morning from my workers who won't appear for work that day. Julie and I always hire more people than we need for just this reason. We're always astounded people won't help themselves. We don't pay high wages, but people can work as many hours as they want. Our few employees who are willing to work often put in 50 hours a week, and their paychecks reflect that. Diana was living with Cheryl and borrowing her car, had no money and no prospects, yet refused to show up at her job.

I've changed the way I handle these situations. I used to get mad and finally just fire people who wouldn't work. But now, I at least attempt to counsel them. It is the most difficult thing I do. In Diana's case, I tried hard to explain that the habits she cultivated in this, her first job, would determine how she fared in life. Working at Hurst Greenery is not the way to fame and fortune, but if you learn to show up and work hard, you have learned the most important lessons any job can teach. My blunter wife told Diana if she didn't start showing up for work on a more regular basis, she would be fired. Neither approach was successful.

> *"Too many people still live in poverty . . . because nobody ever told them that they have to show up for work."*

Cheryl was just as young as Diana when we hired her a decade ago. Her initial performance was not good. We were patient and pointed out her productivity did not justify her salary. She improved and became a truly outstanding employee. The experience she gained here has served her well; she now works for a regional garden center chain and has already been promoted. No job is a dead-end job.

Bad Habits of the Poor

President [Bill] Clinton took his poverty tour [in the summer of 1999], spreading promises of tax incentives and loan guarantees in his wake. An Associated Press story on the President's visit to East Saint Louis led with a description of George Moore, a young man visiting the local unemployment office. He'd lost his $670-a-week job as a dishwasher for oversleeping in the morning.

The article went on to talk about how Moore's lack of skills and education dim his prospects. But Mr. Moore had a job. And lack of education did not cause him to lose it. I have no idea how to solve the urban decay that plagues places like East Saint Louis, but I do know that Moore's prospects would improve dramatically if he bought an alarm clock.

The first step toward preparing workers in poverty-stricken areas for the "twenty-first-century" economy is to instill in them the habits that have served successful people well in the preceding 20 centuries—beginning with prompt and regular appearance at the job site. Our society as a whole suffers from the same failing I have as a supervisor: We find it hard to tell people like Diana what we expect, and harder still to forcefully point out their shortcomings when they fail to perform.

I serve on the board of a small insurance company here in Missouri. We are attempting to install a system of merit pay for our clerical and accounting staff, but it is extremely difficult. Managers are slow to write realistic performance appraisals. Like the school children in Lake Woebegone, everybody that works at our company is above average.

Our society holds no value higher than the refusal to judge others. From President to clerk, we refuse to hold people accountable for their performance, and we lack the courage to make the judgments people like Diana and George Moore so desperately need. When we shirk our responsibilities as managers and voters, we fail poor people in a more profound matter than any lack of government funding or shortage of tax credits and guaranteed loans.

So, we'll spend billions on government housing and high-tech training, drag Fortune 500 executives around the country urging them to build plants in places like East St. Louis, and give false hope to the folks who live in places like the Pine Ridge Indian Reservation. But nobody will point out the obvious: What we lack is character, not government programs. Too many people still live in poverty in these prosperous times simply because nobody ever told them that they have to show up for work.

Unjust Government Policies Contribute to Poverty

by Colette Jay

About the author: *Colette Jay is director of the U.S. Branch of the Fourth World Movement, a volunteer organization that fosters partnerships between families in persistent poverty and other members of society.*

A family wrongfully evicted, another family given a one-way bus ticket by social services to a tiny town in Appalachia, families kept apart by the justice system, children doomed to be left behind. All of this and more comes to mind when asked, "What is the reality facing people who are very poor?" Extreme poverty is often defined by a certain level of income, but it is more complicated than that. Joseph Wresinski, founder of the Fourth World Movement, wrote that, "Chronic poverty results when the lack of basic security simultaneously affects several aspects of people's lives, when it is prolonged, and when it severely compromises people's chances of regaining their rights and of reassuming their responsibilities in the foreseeable future."

Below, we highlight a few of the situations currently faced by families we know. Many aspects of their lives are governed by government policies and funding. One overriding aspect, however, is independent of the government. It is the disrespect with which these families are treated and the exclusion they face from their fellow citizens. While we must work to have good policies with adequate funding, we must also seek to reverse the lack of understanding and negative attitudes non-poor people too often have towards their more disadvantaged neighbors.

Housing Problems in New York City

The Cummings-Reed family (the name has been changed to protect their privacy) knows what it is like to search desperately for an apartment. [In 1997],

Colette Jay, "When Life Is a Struggle—Stories of Those Who Live in Poverty," *Network Connection*, vol. 31, May/June 2003, pp. 8–9. Copyright © 2003 by NETWORK, A National Catholic Justice Lobby, 801 Pennsylvania Ave. SE, Suite 460, Washington, DC, 20003. For membership information, call (202) 547-5556. Reproduced by permission.

the family had to search for months. They finally found an apartment in a neighborhood where they were not too afraid, and where the landlord would accept them and their Section 8 package (government subsidized rental assistance). Their newfound stability did not last long, however.

[In 2003], their current landlord told the family they'd have to leave. He wanted to renovate and charge more rent, or sell the building. (He hadn't maintained the building adequately during their time there.) Then public assistance closed Ms. Reed's case. While she went through the laborious fair-hearing process, it meant weeks of no money, few food stamps and no payment of the public assistance portion of the family's rent. Ms. Reed won the hearing—her benefits should never have been cut—but the landlord had reason to begin eviction proceedings.

While dealing with housing court, continuing hassles with public assistance, and school issues for their sons, the family once again undertook the difficulties of finding affordable housing in New York City. Just like before, it was difficult to find a landlord willing to accept their Section 8 package. Landlords in only minimally decent neighborhoods frown upon or outright reject families on public assistance; they shake their heads at families with teenage children. And those who do accept government rental programs prefer the hefty financial bonuses they receive for housing families from the shelter system, rather than the subsidies they receive through Section 8.

> *"Many aspects of [poor people's] lives are governed by government policies and funding."*

Ms. Reed considered going into the shelter system to have a better chance of getting an apartment but when she went to New York City's Emergency Assistance Unit she changed her mind. The misery, chaos and disrespect she saw there shocked her. There seemed to be hundreds of families waiting for hours to be "assessed." Many were sleeping on the floor, despite a law passed to protect families from having to do so. No food was allowed in the building. To eat, people had to get a pass to go out; if they missed their name being called, they had to restart the process. Most of the staff were either apathetic or hostile. Ms. Reed would not accept the stress and despair of that place for her family. The family of five went to share the one-bedroom apartment of Mr. Cummings' mother.

The family continues to look, on their own and with help from one of our Volunteer Corps members, but time is running out. When Ms. Reed went recently to the Section 8 office, she was told by the caseworker, "This is the last extension I'm giving you." The decision, apparently, was at the discretion of the caseworker with no mention about what Ms. Reed's rights were. The caseworker didn't seem to understand how much time and money Ms. Reed has spent trying to find a place, making phone calls and visiting apartments, nor how much time she has had to spend in court for the eviction proceedings and with school officials to get one of her sons in a special reading program.

Time is also running out because of President [George W.] Bush's proposal to end the Section 8 federal housing assistance and replace it with block grants to the states. We do not know how it will impact the Cummings-Reed family directly, especially if they have not yet found an apartment. While it has the potential to give states more flexibility, flexibility is only positive when everyone is treated with respect. Otherwise, we can only fear this will mean even more difficulties for the Cummings-Reed family and many others to face.

Shifting the Responsibility

In a small town in the mountains of southwestern Virginia, a family has just arrived from Chicago. They know no one, have little money and no place to go. Their bus tickets, given to them by social services in Chicago, were one way. Luckily, they met a woman who has not always had an easy life herself, but who is willing to share what she has and help the family get settled. Perhaps the family thought they would be able to start over here. However, in an area with four times the unemployment rate of the rest of the state, there is little hope the family will have a better life here. Chicago's welfare rolls are down by one, though. . . .

The Challenges Children Face

In New Orleans, as elsewhere, many of the families we know have had a member in jail at one time or another. Guilty or not, these people have rights, but the justice system rarely seems to work in their favor. One mother who is in prison has been unable to see her children for over seven months now because visiting hours are only during the school day. The woman looking after the children doesn't want to subject them to the humiliation of explaining to their teacher why they would be missing school. In another family, one teenage son was arrested and, for lack of space in the juvenile facilities, was kept in the main jail for over a week without once being able to see his mother. Another mother made a two-hour trip to see her son during visiting hours, was told that he couldn't have visitors then and was later criticized by her son's lawyer for not visiting him. . . .

"Multiple, simultaneous challenges [are] faced by families who are very poor."

Initially, despite its inadequacies in certain areas, President Bush's No Child Left Behind Act brought hope that something would change for poor children. The law promised high expectations, qualified teachers, additional tutoring and increased parental involvement. A lack of funding, however, has already made these promises hollow. Children—whose intelligence and creativity we see in our afterschool programs—continue to fail in school. Parents continue to feel looked down upon by teachers and other school staff. We regularly hear from them, "I want to have a teacher who will tell me good things about my child and not just when he has done bad or is acting up in class." Teachers need support too, though, to not feel overwhelmed, especially when teaching children whose lives are so difficult.

The above examples give a good idea of the multiple, simultaneous challenges faced by families who are very poor and the efforts they make to navigate complex systems and overcome poverty. These efforts, however, often go unrecognized by the rest of society. Enacting just and fair policies is the duty of our elected officials, and we must hold them to it. We must also hold ourselves and those around us to our duty, to treat our fellow human beings with respect.

American Immigration Policy Contributes to Poverty

by Samuel Francis

About the author: *Samuel Francis is a nationally syndicated columnist.*

[Since 2001], the discussion of immigration policy in this country has understandably focused on the connection between the mass immigration so beloved by the Open Borders lobby and the terrorism that so pulverized the American psyche [on September 11, 2001]. Nothing has so dramatized the folly of Open Borders than Sept. 11, but despite its importance and its drama, terrorism by immigrants is not the only—or even the main—reason for keeping the borders shut.

The Impact of Third World Immigration

The cultural impact of Third World immigration—on language, on manners, on crime and political institutions—is the main reason to keep American borders tight, but there are economic (and therefore also cultural) reasons, as well. The *New York Times* [in August 2002] specified a few of them.

"The surprising drop in median income in New York City that has puzzled demographers studying the results of the 2000 census appears to be traceable in large part to immigration," the *Times* reported, using 2000 Census Bureau figures. Those parts of the Big Apple in which income dropped just happen to be the same ones where the most immigrants have settled, often in neighborhoods "where long-time residents have moved out and been replaced by immigrants."

The same pattern was apparent in New Jersey, also. There, the biggest jump in income came in Hunterdon County, "a heavily white county at the heart of what has been called the state's flourishing wealth belt. Meanwhile, median incomes dropped in Newark, Paterson and Trenton, and in smaller cities where less educated, less skilled immigrants have moved in."

Nor is it only New York and New Jersey. About 25 percent of the nation's Hispanic population lives below the poverty line, with 27 percent of Puerto Rican families and 24 percent of Mexican families. Only Cubans, 11 percent of whom are in poverty, depart from the norm—mainly because they consist of the Cuban upper classes and their descendants, who felt the brunt of Fidel Castro's "liberation."

Teen-age Latino girls "have the highest teen-age birthrate of all major racial and ethnic groups in the nation," the *Los Angeles Times* reported [in the spring of 2002]. "Recent immigrants make less money, own fewer homes and are less likely to become citizens than foreigners who came to the United States in decades past," the *Houston Chronicle* reported . . . from [a 2001 study conducted by] the Center for Immigration Studies.

Imported Poverty

The Center has estimated that Mexican immigration has reduced the wages of native unskilled workers (mostly black) by some 5 percent. Of course, the only reason these patterns should be "surprising" or that demographers should be "puzzled" is that both the surprised *Times* and the puzzled demographers have swallowed the Big Lies of the Open Border crowd—that more immigrants create wealth and "have saved our cities." What the 2000 Census tells us is that the Big Lie is just that.

But we should not have had to wait for the Census to know that. It ought to be pretty obvious that masses of low-skill, low-income, low-education people from cultures radically different from those of this country or its parent civilization would not typically become millionaires overnight. It should have been obvious that masses of such people would not only not assimilate to a culture (including an economic culture) in which they remained, literally, alien, but also that the presence of millions of them would simply replicate their old culture here.

The reason it wasn't obvious is that the Open Borders lobby has cleverly exploited the myth of Economic Man to insinuate into the American mind the unexamined premise that immigration today means Asian computer geniuses and Korean store owners. There are such immigrants, obviously, but they're not typical of the millions who have entered this country during the last 30 years.

> *"[Third-world] immigrants . . . have imported the culture that impoverished them."*

The Open Borders lobby has also managed to get many Americans to believe that the economic impact of immigration is the only way to evaluate it and the policies that created it. Even by that standard, as the figures cited here show, we'd have to grade it with an "F." But what figures show is seldom the whole truth.

The larger truth is that by importing not only low-skills but also the culture that produced the low skills, the immigrants may endanger the whole cultural foundation of an advanced economy—an economy whose high technology, work ethic, and managerial and organizational skills distinguish it from the burros and grindstones that drag the economies of Latin America, the Middle East, Africa and most of Asia. What we are now beginning to learn the hard way is that the immigrants may not only have imported themselves—they may also have imported the culture that impoverished them and their countries in the first place.

A Variety of Social Factors Causes Homelessness

by the National Coalition for the Homeless

About the author: *The National Coalition for the Homeless is a charity that fights to end homelessness through grassroots organizing, public education, and policy advocacy.*

Two trends are largely responsible for the rise in homelessness over the past 20–25 years: a growing shortage of affordable rental housing and a simultaneous increase in poverty. Below is an overview of current poverty and housing statistics, as well as additional factors contributing to homelessness. . . .

Homelessness and poverty are inextricably linked. Poor people are frequently unable to pay for housing, food, child care, health care, and education. Difficult choices must be made when limited resources cover only some of these necessities. Often it is housing, which absorbs a high proportion of income, that must be dropped. Being poor means being an illness, an accident, or a paycheck away from living on the streets.

In 2000, 11.3% of the U.S. population, or 31.1 million people, lived in poverty. While the number of poor people has decreased a bit in recent years, the number of people living in extreme poverty has increased. In 2000, 39% of all people living in poverty had incomes of less than half the poverty level. This statistic remains unchanged from the 1999 level. Forty percent of persons living in poverty are children; in fact, the 2000 poverty rate of 16.2% for children is significantly higher than the poverty rate for any other age group.

Two factors help account for increasing poverty: eroding employment opportunities for large segments of the workforce, and the declining value and availability of public assistance.

Eroding Work Opportunities

Media reports of a growing economy and low unemployment mask a number of important reasons why homelessness persists, and, in some areas of the

National Coalition for the Homeless, "Why Are People Homeless?" *NCH Fact Sheet #1*, September 2002. Copyright © 2002 by the National Coalition for the Homeless. Reproduced by permission.

country, is worsening. These reasons include stagnant or falling incomes and less secure jobs which offer fewer benefits.

While the last few years have seen growth in real wages at all levels, these increases have not been enough to counteract a long pattern of stagnant and declining wages. Low-wage workers have been particularly hard hit by wage trends and have been left behind as the disparity between rich and poor has mushroomed. To compound the problem, the real value of the minimum wage in 1997 was 18.1% less than in 1979. Although incomes appear to be rising, this growth is largely due to more hours worked—which in turn can be attributed to welfare reform and the tight labor markets. Factors contributing to wage declines include a steep drop in the number and bargaining power of unionized workers; erosion in the value of the minimum wage; a decline in manufacturing jobs and the corresponding expansion of lower-paying service-sector employment; globalization; and increased nonstandard work, such as temporary and part-time employment.

Declining wages, in turn, have put housing out of reach for many workers: in every state, more than the minimum wage is required to afford a one- or two-bedroom apartment at Fair Market Rent. In fact, in the median state a minimum-wage worker would have to work 89 hours each week to afford a two-bedroom apartment at 30% of his or her income, which is the federal definition of affordable housing. Currently, 5 million rental households have "worst case housing needs," which means that they pay more than half their incomes for rent, living in severely substandard housing, or both. The primary source of income for 80% of these households is earnings from jobs. In 1998, this was the case for only 40% of households with worst case housing needs. This represents a 40% increase in working households with worst case housing needs from 1995 to 1999.

The connection between impoverished workers and homelessness can be seen in homeless shelters, many of which house significant numbers of full-time wage earners. A survey of 27 U.S. cities found that over one in four people in homeless situations are employed, a significant increase from 1998. In a number of cities not surveyed by the U.S. Conference of Mayors—as well as in many states—the percentage is even higher.

The future of job growth does not appear promising for many workers: a 1998 study estimated that 46% of the jobs with the most growth between 1994 and 2005 pay less than

> *"Being poor means being an illness, an accident, or a paycheck away from living on the streets."*

$16,000 a year; these jobs will not lift families out of poverty. Moreover, 74% of these jobs pay below a livable wage ($32,185 for a family of four).

Thus, for many Americans, work provides no escape from poverty. The benefits of economic growth have not been equally distributed; instead, they have been concentrated at the top of income and wealth distributions. A rising tide does not lift all boats, and in the United States today, many boats are struggling to stay afloat.

A Decline in Public Assistance

The declining value and availability of public assistance is another source of increasing poverty and homelessness. Until its repeal in August 1996, the largest cash assistance program for poor families with children was the Aid to Families with Dependent Children (AFDC) program. Between 1970 and 1994, the typical state's AFDC benefits for a family of three fell 47%, after adjusting for inflation. The Personal Responsibility and Work Opportunity Reconciliation Act of 1996 (the federal welfare reform law) repealed the AFDC program and replaced it with a block grant program called Temporary Assistance to Needy Families (TANF). Current TANF benefits and Food Stamps combined are below the poverty level in every state; in fact, the median TANF benefit for a family of three is approximately one-third of the poverty level. Thus, contrary to popular opinion, welfare does not provide relief from poverty.

Welfare caseloads have dropped sharply since the passage and implementation of welfare reform legislation. However, declining welfare rolls simply mean that fewer people are receiving benefits—not that they are employed or doing better financially. Early findings suggest that although

> *"Contrary to popular opinion, welfare does not provide relief from poverty."*

more families are moving from welfare to work, many of them are faring poorly due to low wages and inadequate work supports. Only a small fraction of welfare recipients' new jobs pay above-poverty wages; most of the new jobs pay far below the poverty line. These statistics from the Institute for Children and Poverty are particularly revealing:

> In the Institute for Children and Poverty study, 37% of homeless families had their welfare benefits reduced or cut in the last year. More strikingly, in Bucks County and Philadelphia, PA, and Seattle, WA, more than 50% had their benefits reduced or cut . . . Among those who lost their benefits, 20% said they became homeless as a direct result. Additionally, a second study of six states found that between 1997 and 1998, 25% of families who had stopped receiving welfare in the last six months doubled-up on housing to save money, and 23% moved because they could not pay rent.

Moreover, extreme poverty is growing more common for children, especially those in female-headed and working families. This increase can be traced directly to the declining number of children lifted above one-half of the poverty line by government cash assistance for the poor.

As a result of loss of benefits, low wages, and unstable employment, many families leaving welfare struggle to get medical care, food, and housing. Many lose health insurance, despite continued Medicaid eligibility: a recent study found that 675,000 people lost health insurance in 1997 as a result of the federal welfare reform legislation, including 400,000 children. Moreover, over 725,000 workers, laid off from their jobs due to the recession [in 2001 and 2002] lost their health insurance.

In addition, housing is rarely affordable for families leaving welfare for low wages, yet subsidized housing is so limited that fewer than one in four TANF families nationwide lives in public housing or receives a housing voucher to help them rent a private unit. For most families leaving the rolls, housing subsidies are not an option. In some communities, former welfare families appear to be experiencing homelessness in increasing numbers.

> *"Former welfare families appear to be experiencing homelessness in increasing numbers."*

In addition to the reduction in the value and availability of welfare benefits for families, recent policy changes have reduced or eliminated public assistance for poor single individuals. Several states have cut or eliminated General Assistance (GA) benefits for single impoverished people, despite evidence that the availability of GA reduces the prevalence of homelessness.

People with disabilities, too, must struggle to obtain and maintain stable housing. In 1998, on a national average, a person receiving Supplemental Security Income (SSI) benefits had to spend 69% of his or her SSI monthly income to rent a one-bedroom apartment at Fair Market Rent; in more than 125 housing market areas, the cost of a one-bedroom apartment at Fair Market Rent was more than a person's total monthly SSI income.

Presently, most states have not replaced the old welfare system with an alternative that enables families and individuals to obtain above-poverty employment and to sustain themselves when work is not available or possible.

A Lack of Affordable Housing

A lack of affordable housing and the limited scale of housing assistance programs have contributed to the current housing crisis and to homelessness.

The gap between the number of affordable housing units and the number of people needing them has created a housing crisis for poor people. Between 1973 and 1993, 2.2 million low-rent units disappeared from the market. These units were either abandoned, converted into condominiums or expensive apartments, or became unaffordable because of cost increases. Between 1991 and 1995, median rental costs paid by low-income renters rose 21%; at the same time, the number of low-income renters increased. Over these years, despite an improving economy, the affordable housing gap grew by one million. Between 1970 and 1995, the gap between the number of low-income renters and the amount of affordable housing units skyrocketed from a nonexistent gap to a shortage of 4.4 million affordable housing units—the largest shortfall on record.

More recently, the strong economy has caused rents to soar, putting housing out of reach for the poorest Americans. Between 1995 and 1997, rents increased faster than income for the 20% of American households with the lowest incomes. This same study found that the number of housing units that rent for less than $300, adjusted for inflation, declined from 6.8 million in 1996 to 5.5 million in 1998, a 19 percent drop of 1.3 million units. The loss of affordable housing puts even greater numbers of people at risk of homelessness.

The lack of affordable housing has led to high rent burdens (rents which absorb a high proportion of income), overcrowding, and substandard housing. These phenomena, in turn, have not only forced many people to become homeless; they have put a large and growing number of people at risk of becoming homeless. A recent Housing and Urban Development (HUD) study found that 4.9 million unassisted, very low-income households—this is 10.9 million people, 3.6 million of whom are children—had "worst case needs" for housing assistance in 1999. Although this figure seems to be a decrease from 1997, it is misleading since, in the same two-year span, "the number of units affordable to extremely low-income renters dropped between 1997 and 1999 at an accelerated rate, and shortages of housing both affordable and available to these renters actually worsened."

Limited Housing Assistance

Housing assistance can make the difference between stable housing, precarious housing, or no housing at all. However, the demand for assisted housing clearly exceeds the supply: only about one-third of poor renter households receive a housing subsidy from the federal, state, or a local government. The limited level of housing assistance means that most poor families and individuals seeking housing assistance are placed on long waiting lists. From 1996–1998, the time households spent on waiting lists for HUD housing assistance grew dramatically. For the largest public housing authorities, a family's average time on a waiting list rose from 22 to 33 months from 1996 to 1998—a 50% increase. The average waiting period for a Section 8 rental assistance voucher rose from 26 months to 28 months between 1996 and 1998.

> *"The strong economy has caused rents to soar, putting housing out of reach for the poorest Americans."*

Excessive waiting lists for public housing mean that people must remain in shelters or inadequate housing arrangements longer. For instance, in the mid-1990s in New York, families stayed in a shelter an average of five months before moving on to permanent housing. Today, the average stay is nearly a year. Consequently, there is less shelter space available for other homeless people, who must find shelter elsewhere or live on the streets.

A housing trend with a particularly severe impact on homelessness is the loss of single room occupancy (SRO) housing. In the past, SRO housing served to house many poor individuals, including poor persons suffering from mental illness or substance abuse. From 1970 to the mid-1980s, an estimated one million SRO units were demolished. The demolition of SRO housing was most notable in large cities: between 1970–1982, New York City lost 87% of its $200 per month or less SRO stock; Chicago experienced the total elimination of cubicle hotels; and by 1985, Los Angeles had lost more than half of its downtown SRO housing. From 1975 to 1988, San Francisco lost 43% of its stock of low-cost residential hotels; from 1970 to 1986, Portland, Oregon lost 59% of its residential hotels; and from 1971 to 1981, Denver lost 64% of its SRO hotels. Thus the destruction of SRO housing is a major factor in the growth of homelessness in many cities.

Finally, it should be noted that the largest federal housing assistance program is the entitlement to deduct mortgage interest from income for tax purposes. In fact, for every one dollar spent on low income housing programs, the federal treasury loses four dollars to housing-related tax expenditures, 75% of which benefit households in the top fifth of income distribution. Moreover, in 1994 the top fifth of households received 61% of all federal housing benefits (tax and direct), while the bottom fifth received only 18%. Thus, federal housing policy has not responded to the needs of low-income households, while disproportionately benefitting the wealthiest Americans.

> *"Approximately half of all women and children experiencing homelessness are fleeing domestic violence."*

Other Factors

Particularly within the context of poverty and the lack of affordable housing, certain additional factors may push people into homelessness. Other major factors which can contribute to homelessness include the following:

Lack of affordable health care: For families and individuals struggling to pay the rent, a serious illness or disability can start a downward spiral into homelessness, beginning with a lost job, depletion of savings to pay for care, and eventual eviction. In 2000, approximately 38.7 million Americans had no health care insurance. Nearly a third of persons living in poverty had no health insurance of any kind. The coverage held by many others would not carry them through a catastrophic illness.

Domestic violence: Battered women who live in poverty are often forced to choose between abusive relationships and homelessness. In a study of 777 homeless parents (the majority of whom were mothers) in ten U.S. cities, 22% said they had left their last place of residence because of domestic violence. In addition, 34% of cities surveyed by the U.S. Conference of Mayors identified domestic violence as a primary cause of homelessness. Studying the entire country, though, reveals that the problem is even more serious. Nationally, approximately half of all women and children experiencing homelessness are fleeing domestic violence.

Mental illness: Approximately 22% of the single adult homeless population suffers from some form of severe and persistent mental illness. Despite the disproportionate number of severely mentally ill people among the homeless population, increases in homelessness are not attributable to the release of severely mentally ill people from institutions. Most patients were released from mental hospitals in the 1950s and 1960s, yet vast increases in homelessness did not occur until the 1980s, when incomes and housing options for those living on the margins began to diminish rapidly. According to the Federal Task Force on Homelessness and Severe Mental Illness, only 5–7% of homeless persons with mental illness need to be institutionalized; most can live in the community with the appropriate supportive housing options. However, many mentally ill homeless people are unable to obtain access to supportive housing and/or other treatment services. The mental health support services most needed include case management, housing, and treatment.

Addiction disorders: The relationship between addiction and homelessness is complex and controversial. While rates of alcohol and drug abuse are disproportionately high among the homeless population, the increase in homelessness over the past two decades cannot be explained by addiction alone. Many people who are addicted to alcohol and drugs never become homeless, but people who are poor and addicted are clearly at increased risk of homelessness. During the 1980s, competition for increasingly scarce low-income housing grew so intense that those with disabilities such as addiction and mental illness were more likely to lose out and find themselves on the streets. The loss of SRO housing, a source of stability for many poor people suffering from addiction and/or mental illness, was a major factor in increased homelessness in many communities.

Addiction does increase the risk of displacement for the precariously housed; in the absence of appropriate treatment, it may doom one's chances of getting housing once on the streets. Homeless people often face insurmountable barriers to obtaining health care, including addictive disorder treatment services and recovery supports. The following are among the obstacles to treatment for homeless persons: lack of health insurance; lack of documentation; waiting lists; scheduling difficulties; daily contact requirements; lack of transportation; ineffective treatment methods; lack of supportive services; and cultural insensitivity. An in-depth study of 13 communities across the nation revealed service gaps in every community in at least one stage of the treatment and recovery continuum for homeless people.

Homelessness results from a complex set of circumstances which require people to choose between food, shelter, and other basic needs. Only a concerted effort to ensure jobs that pay a living wage, adequate support for those who cannot work, affordable housing, and access to health care will bring an end to homelessness.

Deinstitutionalization of the Mentally Ill Contributes to Homelessness

by Ed Marciniak

About the author: *Ed Marciniak is the president of the Institute of Urban Life at Loyola University in Chicago, Illinois.*

When president Lyndon Johnson declared a "war on poverty" in 1964, the homeless did not appear in the nations' vocabulary, except perhaps as "bums" or "hobos." The visibility of homeless people increased in the late 1960's and early 1970's, when nearly a half-million hospital beds were closed nationwide in state-run mental hospitals, and their occupants were shipped for community care to neighborhood-based institutions. Unfortunately, a great many of the evicted wound up without shelter on city and suburban streets.

Ever since that deinstitutionalization, the number of homeless (both the mentally ill and others) has continued to increase. Approximately two million persons are now homeless at some time during the year, according to the National Law Center on Homelessness and Poverty. New York City alone spends $850 million a year to house and counsel homeless people. Currently, the U.S. Department of Housing and Urban Development provides more than $1 billion yearly to fund programs for them.

Despite today's unprecedented prosperity, homelessness is unlikely to lessen and may even increase. Corroborating such a prediction are two comprehensive surveys released in December 1999 by the U.S. Conference of Mayors and the U.S. Department of Housing and Urban Development. The Conference of Mayors, for example, reported that most of the cities surveyed had reported more requests for emergency shelter.

In many cases, homelessness signals deeper problems. All may qualify as homeless, but many desperately need more than a roof over their heads. Their basic need may not be housing at all. Paradoxically, current public policy at the city and state levels actually generates homelessness. Unless this predicament changes dramatically, no decline in the number of shelterless can be expected.

How then do governmental policy and expenditures shortchange the homeless? Nationwide in the 1960's, there were 500,000 state beds for the mentally ill. Today, there are fewer than 70,000. In the 1950's New York State's mental hospitals housed 93,000 patients; now there are 6,000. Consequently, thousands of mentally ill men and women now stumble along the streets without a home and without the medication they need. What they deserve is a caring residential facility with constructive things to do, help in developing their abilities and assistance with their prescribed medications.

The count of the mentally-ill homeless would be even higher were not large numbers in jails or prisons. In many cities, the local jails has become the community's largest institution for them. Schizophrenics or manic-depressives are more likely to be arrested for conduct related to their ailments than to be granted refuge in mental health facilities. In New York City, for example, nearly 3,000 mentally ill people are behind bars.

> *"Thousands of mentally ill men and women now stumble along the streets without a home and without the medication they need."*

Sixteen percent of the nation's mentally ill are likely to be imprisoned, according to a U.S. Department of Justice study released in 1999. Only a minority of those imprisoned are given treatment. Furthermore, upon release, they are seldom referred to local institutions for medical attention. Many become homeless, deteriorate, are re-arrested and then return to jail.

Another large group of homeless—hard-core drug or alcohol abusers—are also shortchanged. Despite a hard-fought war against drugs, the nations' epidemic of substance abuse thrives. Many users eventually become penniless, helpless and then homeless—especially those with lower incomes. (The Federal Centers for Disease Control and Prevention in Atlanta recently reminded us that cocaine and marijuana use among high schoolers grew steadily during the 1990's before finally tapering off.) Hard-core users willing to kick their drug or alcohol habit by undergoing treatment find their options limited. In most large cities, detoxification centers and halfway houses are understaffed, overcrowded and too few in number.

Also among the homeless are urban vagabonds, drug-addicted down-and-outers, many of whom rebel against a shelter's hospitality requirements for cleanliness and sobriety. These include the Chicagoans removed [in 2000] from the sidewalks of Lower Wacker Drive, where they lived in cardboard boxes or other makeshift shelters. Still others are periodically homeless because of domestic violence, the loss of jobs, death of breadwinner or lack of affordable housing. Among them are runaways and unwed mothers with young children. Many are employed or employable.

A Shift in Attitude

In the meantime, a significant shift is taking place in the public's attitude toward the homeless. Ten years ago the dominating question was: are there enough beds, especially in the winter? New questions are now being advanced. Why have we not succeeded in breaking the cycles of homelessness? A shelter tonight, but what about the rest of the year? Public and private funders want to know whether their dollars make a difference. How many of the homeless are now in more or less permanent housing? How many have jobs? And how many have kicked the habit of substance abuse?

As a result, many city officials now understand that most homeless people require more than a shelter to abandon the city streets. They need not only a bed but also a reason to get out of it. Governments increasingly demand that the shelters they fund do more than supply overnight beds, so that through hands-on counseling and individualized attention, more homeless people will be able to rejoin the urban mainstream. On the other hand, public officials also realize that turning around the lives of the homeless is no cinch and that it takes time.

What initiatives are now being taken to prevent homelessness? In some cities, nonviolent drug offenders who are arrested are given treatment instead of jail sentences. Addicted welfare recipients are required to undergo treatment. More jail wardens, when releasing mentally ill prisoners, now steer them to social agencies for follow-up psychiatric care. Greater efforts are being made to ensure that deadbeat dads (and moms) make their child support payments. Some city employees have become pro-active by going out on the streets trying to persuade the homeless to take advantage of counseling and social services. And nationally and locally, new steps, including rent subsidies, are underway to increase the supply of affordable housing for low-income homeless.

More and more citizens understand that the billions of dollars now being spent annually to imprison the mentally ill and drug addicts could better be used for programs of prevention and treatment. Yet too little is being done to set up additional halfway homes and detoxification centers or to multiply residences for the troubled mentally ill.

While individuals, social institutions and local governments have slowly begun to take steps that could eventually alleviate the nation's homelessness, the problem remains. Current efforts are still too few and too small in scope. Wider and broader initiatives must be mounted to aid the destitute on our streets. We now know what steps should be taken to decrease homelessness in the United States. The question is whether we will take those steps.

Chapter 3

Has Welfare Reform Helped the Poor?

CURRENT **CONTROVERSIES**

Chapter Preface

In the United States, large-scale public assistance programs for the poor—commonly referred to as welfare—began with the Social Security Act of 1935. Responding to Americans' needs during the Great Depression, this act provided federal cash relief to the disabled, widowed, and single-parent families in a program that was later named Aid to Families with Dependent Children (AFDC).

Throughout most of the remainder of the twentieth century, the federal government provided cash aid to the poor—mostly unemployed single mothers and their children—without setting limits on how long families could receive this assistance. Some critics argued that this approach was counterproductive because it allowed the poor to be idle, resulting in a permanent underclass of people living off of welfare checks and feeling no incentive to find work. Others maintained that AFDC provided such meager support to single mothers that it was impossible for them to acquire the education and skills necessary to find work and pull themselves out of poverty. Most policy makers agreed that welfare needed to be reformed in order to reduce—rather than sustain—poverty.

In 1996 President Bill Clinton signed the Personal Responsibility and Work Opportunity Reconciliation Act, a reform measure intended to "end welfare as we know it." The act replaced AFDC with a program called Temporary Assistance to Needy Families (TANF), a system that grants states a set amount of funds to distribute to the poor as well as more authority in determining welfare eligibility. In addition, most adult welfare recipients are now required to find jobs within two years after the beginning of their case, and they are limited to a maximum of five years of assistance in their lifetimes.

Now that several years have passed since the enactment of the 1996 reform, analysts have mixed reviews about its effect on poverty in the United States.

On the one hand, the mandatory work requirements spurred people to leave welfare and take jobs, cutting welfare caseloads in half. Moreover, the rates of child poverty—particularly among minority children and children of single mothers—decreased. Most significantly, reform supporters point out, former welfare recipients who work full-time at low-wage jobs can apply for noncash benefits such as child care, food stamps, and Medicaid. While they may have minimum-wage jobs, the noncash benefits subsidize their incomes and increase their standard of living. "When asked in surveys about life after welfare," states researcher Michael Tanner, "former recipients overwhelmingly respond that their lives are 'easier' off the rolls and that they feel more hopeful than before about their future well-being."

Critics, however, point out that the 1996 welfare reform law requires no detailed reporting from states. This, they argue, results in skewed poverty statistics and inconsistently distributed benefits. Administrative and bureaucratic hassles often discourage low-income families from obtaining noncash assistance like food stamps or transportation subsidies. These families become part of the working poor—with very limited access to food, health care, and adequate housing. "Extreme poverty and deprivation continue in the wake of welfare reform," states Kathy Thornton of NETWORK, a Catholic lobbying organization. "Many welfare 'successes' are soup kitchens, food pantries and health clinics. They are there because people are unable to meet their basic needs." Many critics also predict an increase in homelessness as a growing number of poor families reach their maximum five-year welfare limit.

While supporters of welfare reform celebrate the dramatic decrease in welfare rolls, critics continue to question whether the "new welfare" has truly reduced poverty. The authors in the following chapter present various opinions on this timely topic.

Welfare Reform Benefits Single Mothers

by Christopher Jencks

About the author: *Christopher Jencks is the Malcolm Wiener Professor at Harvard University's Kennedy School of Government and a founder of the* American Prospect, *a liberal journal of opinion.*

When Congress passed the Personal Responsibility and Work Opportunity Reconciliation Act (PRWORA) in 1996, the liberal community was almost unanimous in urging President [Bill] Clinton to veto it. Even people like myself, who had supported Clinton's earlier efforts to "end welfare as we know it," thought that PRWORA went too far. Fortunately for the poor, the first five years of welfare reform inflicted far less economic pain than we had expected.

Now the Bush administration wants even tougher work requirements. Once again, most liberal Democrats think it is a mistake to worry about making every last single mother work when we have not yet ensured that those who already work can provide for their children. Once again, I agree: The administration's proposals are dreadful. But the people who claimed that PRWORA would cause a lot of suffering no longer have much credibility with middle-of-the-road legislators, who see welfare reform as an extraordinary success. If we want to regain credibility we need to admit that welfare reform turned out better than we expected and figure out why that was the case. The usual explanation is simply that the economy did better than anyone expected, but that is only part of the story.

Problems with the Old Welfare System

The traditional liberal position on single mothers was always "more is always better." More meant not only that the government should provide more resources but also that it should impose fewer restrictions on the recipients. The electorate has never accepted this view. Most Americans favor generous programs for people who are doing their best to help themselves. But when the government helps people who seem lazy or irresponsible, Americans tend to see this as rewarding vice. So the less a program asks of its beneficiaries, the less likely Americans are to support it. America's pre-1996 welfare program, Aid to Families with Dependent Children (AFDC), was a perfect example of how this logic plays out politically. It asked almost nothing of single mothers, and it gave them almost no money in return. As a result, everyone hated it.

Nonetheless, welfare-reform efforts achieved relatively little during the 1970s and 1980s. Welfare-rights groups were against requiring single mothers to work, and the liberal wing of the Democratic Party was reluctant to offend these groups, partly for fear of seeming racist. The labor market was soft, centrists feared that single

> *"The first five years of welfare reform inflicted far less economic pain than we had expected."*

mothers would not be able to find work in the private sector, and the right was against spending public money to provide jobs. Ambitious politicians came to see welfare reform as the Vietnam of domestic policy: a quagmire to be avoided at almost any cost. And because the welfare rolls were roughly constant from 1975 to 1989, the problem just simmered.

In 1991, with the welfare rolls rising rapidly, Bill Clinton decided that running against AFDC would be a good way to position himself as a "new" Democrat. As president, he set up a task force to propose a new system. By then the Democratic Party was deeply divided on welfare. Some supported a fundamental change, usually because they thought the only way to get more support for single mothers was to insist that the mother go to work. But many traditional liberals remained skeptical about serious work requirements. They saw the least-competent recipients as incapable of doing almost anything, and they could not imagine a system that drew a clear line between those who could work and those who could not. Clinton's 1994 proposals therefore needed Republican support to pass. By then the Republicans were more interested in humiliating Clinton than in reforming welfare, so his relatively generous version of welfare reform was stillborn.

Temporary Assistance to Needy Families

After the Republicans gained control of Congress, they crafted a series of more draconian welfare-reform bills, which most liberals opposed. But after vetoing two such bills, Clinton signed the third. PRWORA replaced AFDC with Temporary Assistance for Needy Families (TANF). Under TANF, states could redesign welfare in almost any way they wanted, setting their own eligibility rules, work requirements, and time limits. TANF did establish federal time limits, but if states wanted to get around those limits they could do so by shuffling funds between programs.

The 1996 legislation was also a powerful symbolic statement. It made clear that America was no longer committed, even in principle, to supporting women who wanted to be full-time mothers. Anyone who wants to have children must either work or find a partner who will work. (The disabled are an exception, but "disability" is quite narrowly defined.) Single mothers judged capable of working can get short-term cash assistance from the government, but they cannot expect long-term assistance unless they have a job, and they cannot expect the government to find them one.

When this legislation was adopted, its opponents made four predictions:

- Many mothers would not be able to find jobs when they hit their TANF time limit;
- Even mothers who found jobs would seldom earn enough to support their family;
- Forcing unmarried mothers to work would not reduce unwed motherhood or discourage divorce; and
- There would not be enough good child care, so more children would be neglected.

What actually happened was rather different.

Work

When PRWORA passed, skeptics argued that there would not be enough jobs to go around. [Table 1] shows that the proportion of single mothers who had worked at some point during the year rose from 73 percent in 1995 to 84 percent in 2000, while the proportion who had worked throughout the year rose from 48 percent to 60 percent. These were unprecedented increases: Nothing similar had happened during any earlier boom, and nothing similar happened among married mothers in the late 1990s.

PRWORA's critics often attribute these gains to the unusually tight labor market between mid-1997 and mid-2001. Some have suggested that unemployment among single mothers will rise sharply now that the labor market has gone soft. Some rise is inevitable in a recession, but the proportion of single mothers with jobs will not return to its 1995 level unless the recession gets much, much worse.

The unemployment rate for single mothers is normally about twice the rate for the labor force as a whole. In March 2001, for example, the overall unemployment rate was 4.3 percent but the rate for single mothers was 8.1 percent. The overall unemployment rate reached 6 percent in April

"The unemployment rate for single mothers fell between 1995 and 2000."

2002, so the rate for single mothers was probably just under 12 percent. That is surely causing a lot of suffering. But the fraction of single mothers with jobs is still far higher than it was before PRWORA.

The critics were right when they said that not all those who leave welfare would find work. Between 1994 and 2000, welfare receipt among single mothers fell from 32 percent to 15 percent, a 17-point drop; employment among single mothers, meanwhile, rose only 11 or 12 points. The question, though, is how many single mothers who wanted jobs failed to find them. The chart shows that the unemployment rate for single mothers fell between 1995 and 2000, which hardly suggests that the labor market was awash in single mothers unable to find work. Of course, workers only get counted as unemployed if they say they are currently looking for work. Some who left welfare presumably had looked earlier, found nothing, grown discouraged, and stopped looking.

"Most single mothers have multiple sources of income, and their economic status has clearly improved since 1996."

Income

When PRWORA was being debated, its opponents often argued that even if single mothers found work they would seldom earn enough to support themselves. If single mothers had to depend entirely on their own wages, this would often have been true. But most single mothers have multiple sources of income, and their economic status has clearly improved since 1996.

The official federal poverty rate among single mothers, was 43 percent at the end of the 1980s expansion, 42 percent when PRWORA passed, and 33 percent in 2000. The drop among black single mothers was even larger. Poverty has probably risen [since 2001], but the rate for 2001 is almost certain to be lower than the rate for 1996. If the overall unemployment rate stays near 6 percent, single mothers are unlikely to experience as much material hardship in this recession as they did in the last one. A severe recession could be another story.

Even before the current recession began, the Center on Budget and Policy Priorities had reported that the poorest single mothers were doing worse than they had before PRWORA passed. But census data on the poorest of the poor are

Table 1. The percentage of single mothers who work has soared, but the percentage who get welfare has fallen even more.

	1995	2000
Worked at least one week during the year	73	84
Worked throughout the year	48	60
Unemployment rate (March 1996 vs. March 2001)	10	8
Received welfare in an average month	33	15

Sources: Welfare data are from the U.S. Department of Health and Human Services. Employment data and counts of single mothers are from tabulations by Joseph Swingle based on the March Current Population Surveys.

problematic for a variety of technical reasons. Such data should never be trusted unless they are consistent with other evidence. If deep poverty had really increased between 1995 and 2000, for example, one would have expected more single mothers to move in with relatives. Census surveys showed no such increase. Likewise, an increase in deep poverty should have meant that more single mothers had trouble feeding their families. Yet the Agriculture Department's annual reports on its food-security surveys showed a fairly steady decline in the proportion of single mothers reporting food shortages, hunger, and related problems. My own work with Joseph Swingle and Scott Winship shows the same thing.

Help for Low-Wage Workers

So why were the prophets of doom wrong? One answer is that almost everyone underestimated the extent to which government support for the poor was being redirected to people with jobs. Soon after Clinton took office in 1993, he persuaded Congress to expand the Earned Income Tax Credit (EITC). Today the EITC distributes more money to working parents than AFDC ever gave to mothers who stayed at home. For a minimum-wage worker with two children, the EITC means a 40 percent increase in annual earnings. More aggressive child-support enforcement has increased some working mothers' incomes even further. Extending Medicaid coverage to some of the working poor has also reduced some mothers' out-of-pocket medical spending, although much remains to be done in this regard.

TANF also gave states block grants that did not shrink as the welfare rolls shrank and allowed states to use these grants for child-care subsidies, which made it much easier for single mothers to survive on what they earned in low-wage jobs. Unfortunately, these subsidies are now in jeopardy, partly because the recession is putting pressure on state budgets and partly because the administration wants to force states to use their TANF money in other ways.

The net result of these changes is that the old "welfare state" is becoming what one might call a "wage-subsidy state," in which government assistance is tied to employment. By asking more of those who get government largesse, the new wage-subsidy

"Children are now a little better off than they were in 1996."

system has substantially reduced political hostility to public spending on the poor. This is especially true at the state level. (In Washington the hard right is still riding high, and the Democrats remain reluctant to oppose the Bush administration even when it tries to limit states' ability to run welfare.)

Welfare Mothers

But what about mothers who left welfare and did not find regular work? Many of these women are clearly struggling, but they are doing better than most of PRWORA's critics expected. They have not benefited from welfare reform, but it has been hard to find much evidence that their position deteriorated, at least prior to last September [2001].

One reason PRWORA's critics were too pessimistic about such mothers' prospects may have been that they were fooled by their own linguistic conventions. When we describe people as welfare mothers, we inevitably begin to see them mainly as people who get a check from the government every month. In reality, however, this check is hardly ever large enough to support the recipient's family. In their book *Making Ends Meet*, Kathryn Edin and Laura Lein reported that welfare checks typically covered about 40 percent of the recipient's expenses. Some of the rest came from food stamps; most of it came from relatives, boyfriends, and working off the books. Edin and Lein's data were gathered in the early 1990s, but the same pattern probably holds today.

> *"Welfare reform has turned out far better than most liberals expected."*

When times are good, family members can be more generous and a mother has a better chance of finding off-the-books work. Boyfriends also earn more in good times, which may be one reason why more single mothers reported live-in boyfriends during the late 1990s. The value of an economic boom to a single mother depends, however, on current norms about how money should be spent. When incomes rose in the late 1980s, a lot of the money that flowed into poor neighborhoods ended up in drug dealers' pockets. When incomes rose in the late 1990s, expenditures on drugs were apparently falling, so more of the new money was available for food, rent, and fixing the TV.

Marriage

The idea that sending checks to unmarried mothers will encourage unwed motherhood and divorce has always seemed self-evident to most Americans. But back in 1996 it was hard to find much statistical evidence for this view. Single parenthood was becoming more common in all rich countries, regardless of how they organized their welfare system. And while welfare benefits varied a lot from one American state to the next, neither the proportion of children born out of wedlock nor the proportion of older children living with an unmarried mother appeared to correlate with benefit levels. When welfare reform was being debated in the mid-1990s, I do not recall hearing a single reputable scholar argue that changing the welfare system was likely to have much effect on marriage rates. I certainly expected no such effect. Even Charles Murray, who believed that welfare had played a role in the spread of single-parent families, felt that something more draconian than PRWORA would be needed to reverse the trend.

Since 1996 both the scholarly consensus and the facts on the ground have changed. Recent research suggests that welfare policy may, in fact, exert some effect on family structure. Furthermore, the spread of single-parent families has stopped. The proportion of mothers raising children without a husband had increased steadily between 1960 and 1996 (from 11 percent to 28 percent). But after March 1997, the proportion began to fall. By March 2001 it was down to 26.6 percent. That was hardly a revolution, but it cut the number of single mothers by half a million.

The proportion of children born to unmarried mothers is still inching up, but the increase since 1995 has been tiny. A study by Richard Bavier of the U.S. Office of Management and Budget suggests that women who have children out of wedlock are now marrying in greater numbers. We do not know whether these mothers are marrying their child's father or someone else. That is important, because children who grow up with a stepfather fare no better in adolescence or early adulthood than children who grow up with a single mother, even though the stepfather's presence substantially increases their family's income.

Children

When PRWORA passed, its critics (including me) worried about how it would affect children. In material terms, children are now a little better off than they were in 1996. Children's psychological well-being is probably more important, but it is also harder to measure. A single mother who works full time obviously has less time for her children, and exhaustion may make her more irritable or more punitive. But the long-term effects of a single mother working remain uncertain and controversial. A lot probably depends on what the mother's job is really like, what it pays, and how flexible it is to family needs.

When mothers enter the labor market, however, their children's child-care arrangements become less stable. Government subsidies appear and disappear unpredictably. The women who provide child care for unskilled working mothers are often unreliable. Mothers often have to take either temporary jobs or jobs with unpredictable hours, and they usually have to change their child-care arrangements when their hours change. Children hate this kind of instability. Whether it causes long-term damage, however, remains unclear.

> *"Shifting government largesse toward those who work was a good idea."*

On balance, welfare reform has turned out far better than most liberals expected. Most Americans now see it as one of the great successes of the 1990s. Instead of remaining wedded to the idea that PRWORA was a bad idea because it was a supported by the lunatic right, liberals need to rethink. My own conclusions are three:

• Telling prospective parents that they would have to take primary responsibility for supporting themselves and their children was a good idea, because 60 years of experience showed that no other approach to reducing family poverty could win broad political support in America.

• Shifting government largesse toward those who work was a good idea, because it helped erase the stigma of single motherhood and made more resources available to single mothers and their children.

• Turning welfare over to the states was a really good idea, because most states currently take a less ideological view of single mothers' problems than does Congress.

Someday, of course, Congress may also show renewed interest in problem solving. At the moment, however, most states' approach to helping poor families is more pragmatic than Washington's, and the new emphasis on helping low-wage workers has created a significantly better system than we had in 1996.

Welfare Reform Is a Success

by George W. Bush

About the author: *George W. Bush is the forty-third president of the United States.*

Editor's Note: The following viewpoint is excerpted from President George W. Bush's remarks to welfare-to-work graduates at the White House on June 10, 2002.

All of you here today who have gone from welfare to work really represent courage and strength. And I want to thank you for your examples of what is possible and for your stories of success. You've earned independence and the respect of your families and your communities, the respect of your President. I congratulate you—I want to congratulate you on using and utilizing your God-given talents to their fullest. So, welcome.

I want to welcome Tommy Thompson, who's the Secretary of Health and Human Sciences. Tommy, thank you for being here. He's a former Governor—nothing wrong with former Governors. [Laughter] But Tommy has been a leader in welfare reform, which is really a leader in helping people. He did a great job as the Governor of Wisconsin. He's doing a great job here in Washington. Thank you, Tommy. . . .

The Historic Welfare Reform Law

The people in this room who have overcome the obstacles have obviously known some really tough times, starting with the fact that the hardest job in America is a single mom. That's the hardest work. People have overcome incredible odds and obstacles and hurdles. But thanks to courage and determination and hard work—in many cases, prayer—you've turned your lives around, and you're strong, proud, successful women, and we want to thank you for that—and strong, proud, successful men, I might add.

George W. Bush, "Remarks to Welfare-to-Work Graduates," *Weekly Compilation of Presidential Documents*, vol. 38, June 10, 2002, p. 958.

The historic welfare reform passed by Congress in 1996 helped many Americans find dignity and self-respect. And that's what we're here to talk about. We're not only here to talk about the lives that have been changed but law and how to make the '96 law work better. And the '96 law worked well because of the—much of it had to do with the work requirement in the law. It basically said, you've got to work. In order to be independent and free, you've got to work, and we want to help you find work. That's what the law said.

The statistics are strong about how successful the '96 law was. At the time, however, it was quite controversial. I wasn't here. I was working

> *"People have overcome incredible odds and obstacles and hurdles."*

with Tommy, trying to get the law passed from the perspective of a Governor. But there was one study, for example—to show you how controversial the bill was—that said, at least a million children would be cast into poverty by the welfare reform law—if it passed, if the '96 bill passed, that a million children would be thrown into poverty.

Well, whoever did that study probably is out of work—at least I hope so—[laughter]—because the truth is, there are 5.4 million fewer people in poverty today than in '96, and there are 2.8 million fewer children living in poverty than in '96. Anyway you look at it, the bill has been really successful.

"The Real Success"

The real success, though, is not found in the numbers. The real success has been found in the number of lives that have been changed. It's one thing to talk about reducing welfare rolls, and that's fine. But the most important thing is the number of lives that have been saved and enriched. That's the most important part about the '96 law and its consequences.

Maria Medellin, de mi estado de Texas—from the State of Texas—is here, and she is one type of story. She's been working for UPS, Big Brown, now for 3 years. When she first came to UPS, she was a single mom on welfare, raising two sons. She needed extra income and benefits to support her family, so she started working at UPS for $8.50 an hour, and then she was promoted. And now she is a recruiter, she's a boss. She's enrolled in college, and she's going to get her degree in 3 years.

Maria says this about her journey and about her struggles: "It was a challenge to overcome the statistic of being a single minority female with two children on welfare. UPS is the foundation that has allowed me to be where I am today. Being able to raise my children and provide for them is my greatest source of pride. Just showing my children that I'm strong enough and can succeed is more than enough for me."

Maria, congratulations.

And there are a lot of people with stories like Maria's. The great thing about the subject we're talking about today is, there are Marias all across America and right here in this room.

And so the fundamental question is, How can we continue this progress? What can we do to continue to make America a better place? As you know, we struggle hard to keep America secure, and we're going to. We will win the war on terror and keep us free. But as we fight for our security, we also must work to make America a better place. And where we find people who've lost hope, we must work to provide hope. And where we find pockets of despair, we must work—all of us work—to eradicate pockets of despair. And one way to continue to make sure. America is a hopeful place, a better place, is to work on a new reauthorization bill for welfare that continues to make progress to help people. That's what we've got to do.

Keeping High Standards

The bill in '96 is up: it's kind of run out of its time. And so it's now time for Congress to come together and pass another measure. And the debate's going to be, What do we do? How do we make it? What do we do? The House has already answered the question by passing a law that really makes sure that work is still an integral part of welfare reform.[1] Work and family are integral parts of welfare reform. I might add.

Here's what I think ought to happen: I think the Senate ought to pass a bill that has the same principles embodied in the House bill. And it

> *"The historic welfare reform passed by Congress in 1996 helped many Americans find dignity and self-respect."*

says that rather than lowering standards, we need to keep high standards in America, particularly when it comes to what we expect in terms of work.

We want 70 percent of the people on welfare working by the next 5 years. That's what we want. We don't want to reduce the number of people that should be working in America, because we understand how important work is to the future of every citizen. We want to raise the standard and raise the bar. And that means 40-hour workweeks. That's what work [is]—that's the definition of work.

Now, I recognize there are a lot of people that need help, and so within the 40-hour workweeks there are credits for education and vocational training, to help people help themselves. A work requirement isn't punishment. A work requirement is part of liberation in our society. But in order to make sure that people are able to work, we want to make sure there is ample training and ample education, to give people the chance they want. And that's what this bill— and that's what this vision for a better welfare reform bill talks about.

---

1. As this volume went to press, the Senate had not ratified the House bill. However, Congress extended the benefits provided by the 1996 Welfare Reform Law until a reauthorized welfare bill could be passed.

And then, of course, there is the issue of money, and that's always a big debate here in Washington, DC. [Laughter] It seems like you can never spend enough. And so one of the things I decided to do was to be wise about how we spent—the amount of money we spent in the welfare appropriations. I thought it made sense to keep the level of welfare spending the same as it has been, which really doubles the amount of money available for States to spend, because the caseload has declined in half. So if you've get the same amount of money and the caseload has declined in half, you've got double the money available for people you're trying to help.

> *"There are 5.4 million fewer people in poverty today than in [1996]."*

And that ought to be ample money for the States to help people with education, vocational training, to help people help themselves. And so I'm confident the amount of money we've got in the bill is more than adequate to meet the needs and to help meet our goals of work and money available to help—to help the 2 million families who are still on welfare rolls. And that's the goal, is to help as many as we possibly can achieve independence and dignity and work.

I think it's important for Members of Congress to talk to the people who—and listen to the people who've succeeded under the current law, who have actually become independent, from Government, and what it means to their lives. They ought to listen to the Marias and the people who I've had the honor of talking to, as they decide how best to help people. They ought to listen to the stories, and they ought to be hopeful and optimistic about what is possible in America. People who are pessimistic about the future lower standards. People who are optimistic raise the standards, because we believe in the best.

The Media Downplay the Benefits of Welfare Reform

by Richard Noyes

About the author: *Richard Noyes is the director of the Media Research Center's Free Market Project.* He is also coeditor of Dollars & Nonsense: Correcting the News Media's Top Economic Myths.

[Several] years ago, much of the news media—particularly the journalists who work at the three major broadcast networks and leading newspapers such as the *New York Times*—couldn't get enough of the story about the historic welfare reform law that a Republican Congress passed and Democratic President Bill Clinton signed.

According to a careful media analysis, the dominant print and electronic news outlets relied overwhelmingly on the pessimistic predictions of "welfare advocates" and cast welfare reform as a dangerous gamble. Sound bite after sound bite warned of the potential harm as politicians ended the system that guaranteed cash assistance to poor families with children.

This year [2002], all indications are that Congress will vote to reauthorize the law, creating a new welfare reform that in its sweep will strongly resemble the one passed in 1996.[1] But apart from whatever legislation is eventually enacted, what may be most striking about the current welfare debate may be the remarkable absence of journalistic interest in the topic. In fact, the news media's silence speaks volumes, testifying to the emergence of a broad new consensus surrounding a law that was vilified by opponents when it was originally passed.

An Obvious Success

"Welfare reform has been an obvious success," the *New York Times* admitted in an April 8, [2002], editorial, even as the newspaper cautioned against Presi-

---

1. As this volume went to press, Congress had not reauthorized the welfare reform law but had extended the benefits enacted in 1996 until a new bill could be passed.

Richard Noyes, "Silence on Welfare Reform," *World & I*, vol. 17, July 2002, pp. 64–69. Copyright © 2002 by News World Communications, Inc. Reproduced by permission.

dent George W. Bush's proposals to increase work requirements on states. (Of course, the fact that the *Times* and some policy studies suggest welfare reform has been a success to date does not mean that it has truly solved the problem of poverty-stricken parents who desperately need help. Social problems are infinitely complex, and a policy that appears to work for a time may fail over the long haul or create new problems never foreseen.)

Six years earlier, the *Times* editors had blasted the very same legislation as "atrocious," predicting it would only add to the misery of the poor. "This is not reform, it is punishment," the *Times* wrote on August 1, 1996, adding that "the [Clinton] administration's staff estimates that [the bill's] provisions will throw a million more children into poverty."

> *"Journalists apparently rejected conservative arguments that the reformed welfare system would do a better job of leading people out of poverty."*

The three broadcast networks have hardly mentioned [the 2002] welfare debate, continuing a pattern of silence that began long before [the September 11, 2001, terrorist attacks] lifted national security to the top of America's news agenda. When the networks do mention welfare reform, it is to acknowledge that the ideological battle of the mid-1990s will not be reprised. "The big debate as to whether or not welfare recipients should be required to work, that's over," ABC White House reporter Terry Moran informed his audience on February 26, [2002]. "Across the political spectrum, there's agreement that welfare reform has worked."

"Dreadful and Terrible"?

[In 1996], it was a very different story, as the media gave favored treatment to the arguments of welfare reform's critics. Supporters of the new welfare reform law condemned welfare as a tried and failed government attempt to fight poverty. They argued that instead of promoting work and self-sufficiency by providing temporary assistance to needy families, the decades-old Aid to Families with Dependent Children actually trapped the poor in a system that encouraged dependency and illegitimacy, even as the ranks of those below the poverty line swelled. Their proposed remedy: new federal welfare laws that would encourage states to experiment with alternatives that would limit benefits and impose work requirements. After he rejected two other similar bills, Clinton announced on July 31, 1996, that he would sign the third welfare reform bill.

Antireform activists, such as those at the liberal Children's Defense Fund (CDF), declared that the new law would be a disaster, and the mass media trumpeted their views. "There's going to be a million children thrust into poverty by this bill," the CDF's Debbie Weinstein warned on the *CBS Evening News* on August 22, 1996, the day welfare reform became law. The *New York Times* carried the condemnation of CDF President Marian Wright Edelman, who declared that ending the guarantee of a federal welfare check to those in need will leave "a moral blot on [Clinton's] presidency and on our nation that will never be forgotten."

The liberal criticism of the Democratic president was predicated on the assumption that welfare reform would fail. Pundits who were generally sympathetic toward Clinton declared outrage at his complicity in making welfare reform law. Correctly predicting that the president would not veto a third welfare reform measure, panelist Margaret Carlson declared on CNN's *Capital Gang* on July 27, 1996, that "the welfare bill is still a terrible bill! The only reason Clinton would sign it is because the Republicans are pushing him into a corner. He said he would end welfare as we know it; he's going to end welfare and bring in something dreadful and terrible and awful for political advantage!"

At the 1996 Democratic National Convention, network reporters used words like "betrayal" as they probed the depths of liberal anger. "You voted against the welfare reform bill," CNN's Wolf Blitzer reminded Sen. Carol Mosley-Braun (D-Illinois) during a convention interview. "Do you feel that he sort of betrayed some of those values that you expressed? How can you go forward now and support him after his decision to sign that welfare reform bill into law?"

"Does anyone else find it unnerving," Jack White wrote in *Time*'s September 2, 1996, issue, "that only days before Bill Clinton signed a welfare-reform law that will plunge more than a million children into of-

> *"There are 4.2 million fewer people living in poverty today than there were [in 1996]."*

ficial poverty, he marked his fiftieth birthday with glitzy celebrations in New York City that added $10 million to his party's bulging campaign war chest? Shades of Marie Antoinette, Newt Gingrich and Jesse Helms."

Many leading journalists apparently rejected conservative arguments that the reformed welfare system would do a better job of leading people out of poverty. "In light of the new welfare reform bill, do you think the children need more prayers than ever before?" Bryant Gumbel, then with NBC, asked the CDF's Edelman on the September 23, 1996, *Today* show.

Tallying the Media Scorecard

Reporters can betray their bias on an issue by the types of questions they ask and the experts whose views they solicit. In 1996, of course, journalists could not know whether experience would ultimately vindicate welfare reform's opponents or its supporters. But most of the media elite apparently did not trust that the proposed changes would, in fact, improve the lives of most aid recipients; if they did, they probably would have shown increasing frustration at those who lobbied against the bill's enactment, as they did with opponents of the highly touted campaign-finance reform law passed in 2002.

Instead, the airwaves were filled with stories about the potentially damaging consequences of welfare reform, indicating that journalists perceived the story to be one of the new challenges to the nation's poor, not about a genuine effort to provide more meaningful assistance. "Once the welfare bill becomes law, millions of Americans will find their lives starting to change in startling and unwelcome ways," then-CBS anchor Paula Zahn asserted on the July 31, 1996, *CBS Evening News* after Clinton's declaration that he would sign the bill.

> *"There are nearly two million fewer hungry children today than at the time welfare reform was enacted."*

That night on ABC's *Nightline*, fill-in anchor Chris Wallace told Health and Human Services Secretary Donna Shalala, "You find yourself now in the position of being praised by Newt Gingrich, at the same time Sen. Pat Moynihan calls this the most brutal piece of social policy since Reconstruction. Doesn't that make you the slightest bit nervous?"

"Welfare reform could leave Los Angeles as penniless as the poor who line up each day for public assistance," Mike Boettcher stated on the August 1, 1996, *NBC Nightly News*. That same evening, his CBS counterpart, Bill Whitaker, similarly warned that "in Los Angeles, America's dream factory, many local politicians are calling the welfare reform bill a nightmare." Whitaker and Boettcher were typical, as the media stressed welfare reform's peril for the poor, not its promise.

Fast-forward to 2001. As the welfare law passed its fifth anniversary, the Heritage Foundation's Robert Rector and Patrick Fagan released *The Good News About Welfare Reform*, a research report detailing welfare reform's track record. Instead of "plunging more than a million children into official poverty," as journalists such as White predicted, there are now 2.3 million fewer children living in poverty than there were in 1996, according to Rector and Fagan, with the strongest improvements among black children. Overall, the Heritage paper reported, "there are 4.2 million fewer people living in poverty today" than there were five years ago. (While these statistics are of course heartening, they may overlook all manner of beneath-the-radar problems, such as the durability of the families' escape from poverty and the psychological effects on children of their single mothers having to spend most of the day at work.)

The media predicted that welfare reform would mean more hunger. "For the first time in decades, the federal government will no longer guarantee open-ended help to the poor," *CBS Evening News* anchor Harry Smith noted on Thanksgiving Day, 1996. "This could mean hunger in America will grow, even in places famous for food and plenty of it." On January 11, 1998, *NBC Nightly News* Sunday anchor Dawn Fratangelo, introducing a story by Roger O'Neil, similarly insisted that welfare reform meant empty stomachs: "While many former recipients may be working, often there is not enough money for one basic need—food."

In his report, O'Neil warned about "the dark side of welfare reform." He stated that "the demand for food is now greater than the supply. Those who serve the poor worry about empty shelves if welfare reform continues to leave the poor hungry, even if they have a job." That was in 1998.

As Rector and Fagan reported [in 2002], "According to the U.S. Department of Agriculture, there are nearly two million fewer hungry children today than at the time welfare reform was enacted."

Uninterested in Good News?

On August 12, 2001, a front-page story in the *New York Times* revealed that "five years after Congress overhauled welfare laws, with the intention of creating more two-parent families, the proportion of poor children living in households with two adults is on the rise, two studies say." Reporter Blaine Harden went on to note that "while the sustained economic boom of the 1990s probably supported these trends, including the increase in two-parent families, there is considerable agreement, even among skeptical policy analysts, that welfare change deserves considerable credit."

It's often true that ABC, CBS, and NBC crib their story ideas from the *New York Times'* front page, but not this time. A weekend edition of the *CBS Evening News* anchored by Russ Mitchell briefly mentioned the *Times* report, as did *CBS Sunday Morning* anchor Charles Osgood. ABC and NBC skipped the news altogether. As with so much involving welfare reform, critics of the new law made headlines with their dire prognostications [several] years ago, while the good news about welfare reform's achievements has received, at best, only incidental media coverage.

But after a heated national debate such as in 1996, it would seem reasonable to expect the national media to document the actual performance of a highly controversial policy such as welfare reform. If nothing else, such reporting could at least provide news organizations with a useful "reality check" of their own reporting. For instance, reporters showed deep skepticism of claims that more restrictive welfare rules would be beneficial to recipients. But a research report published in February [2002] by June O'Neill and Anne Hill, both economics professors at Baruch College at the City University of New York, found that welfare reform has had a profoundly positive effect on the lives of women. "Between passage of the act and June 2001," they wrote, "the number of families on welfare declined by 53 percent. Contrary to the expectations of many welfare reform critics, most of the women heading these families went to work."

> *"Welfare reform has had a profoundly positive effect on the lives of women."*

That's also what Rector and Fagan found: "In the half-decade since the welfare reform law was enacted . . . overall poverty, child poverty, black child poverty, poverty of single mothers, and child hunger have substantially declined. Employment of single mothers increased dramatically and welfare rolls plummeted. The share of children living in single-mother families fell, and more important, the share of children living in married-couple families grew, especially among black families."

The news media play an important role in public policy debates, and reporters serve the public well when they challenge each side with the toughest questions of their opponents. During the welfare debate [of 1996], it would have been incomplete and biased for journalists to omit or downplay the arguments of liberals who feared that welfare reform would harm poor families, just as it was unfair to deemphasize the arguments of conservatives that reform would be an improvement over an old-style welfare program that had failed to fight poverty and improve lives.

The problem then was that too many journalists seemed to accept the liberals' partisan arguments and predictions as unassailable fact, rather than one side of a complicated story—a complexity that may ultimately bear out the concerns of liberals. As much as any major story in recent years, the media's coverage of welfare reform illustrates the need for journalists to remain fair and balanced in their coverage of ideological issues. Otherwise, they risk losing credibility when the "news" they present their audiences cannot stand the test of time.

Welfare Reform Has Not Helped the Poor

by Evelyn Z. Brodkin

About the author: *Evelyn Z. Brodkin is an associate professor at the School of Social Service Administration and a lecturer in the Law School of the University of Chicago.*

There were few mourners at welfare's funeral. In fact, its demise was widely celebrated when congressional Republicans teamed up with a majority of their Democratic colleagues and then-president Bill Clinton to enact a new welfare law in 1996. The law ended the sixty-one-year-old federal commitment to aid poor families and ushered in a commitment to lower welfare rolls and put recipients to work.

To many politicians and the public, anything seemed preferable to the widely discredited program known as Aid to Families with Dependent Children (AFDC). Conservatives were sure that the new welfare would pull up the poor by their bootstraps and redeem them through the virtues of work. Liberals set aside their misgivings, hoping that work would redeem the poor politically and open opportunities to advance economic equality.

More than six years later, the demise of the old welfare remains largely unlamented. But what to make of the changes that have occurred in the name of reform? Often, laws produce more smoke than fire, intimating big change, but producing little. Not this time. In ways both apparent and not fully appreciated, welfare reform has reconfigured both the policy and political landscape. Some of these changes can evoke nostalgia for the bad old days of welfare unreformed.

Reconsidering Welfare's Fate

An immediate consequence of the new law was to defuse welfare as a hot political issue. There's little attention to it these days—apart from some five million parents and children who rely on welfare to alleviate their poverty (and the policy analysts who pore over mountains of data to calculate how it "works").

Legislators have shown no appetite for restarting the welfare wars of prior years. And is it any wonder? The news about welfare has looked good—at least, superficially. Caseloads have plummeted since implementation of the new welfare, dropping 57 percent between 1997 and 2001. Some smaller states essentially cleared their caseloads, with Wyoming and Idaho proudly announcing reductions of 88.9 percent and 85.1 percent, respectively. Even states with large, urban populations have cut caseloads by one-half to three-quarters.

As an issue, welfare ranked among the top five items of interest to the public in 1995 and 1996. But in recent years, it has almost dropped off the Gallup charts. Other polls show that, among respondents who are aware of welfare reform, more than 60 percent think it's working well. Meanwhile, the nation has moved on to other concerns: terrorism, Iraq, the economy. Why reopen the welfare issue now? . . .

> *"Pushing welfare decision making to the state and local level has never been good for the poor."*

Welfare merits a close look because battles over welfare policy have often been a bellwether of broader political developments. Welfare policy was near the forefront of sixties social activism, one of the banners under which the urban poor, minorities, and other disaffected groups successfully pressed for greater government intervention on behalf of social and economic equality. For the national Democratic Party, the politics of poverty fit an electoral strategy aimed at mobilizing urban and minority voters. Although the expansion of welfare proved to be temporary and limited, the politics of poverty produced federal initiatives that had broad and lasting impact, among them Medicaid, food stamps, earned income tax credits, and programs to aid schools in poor communities.

Attacks on welfare marked the beginning of a conservative mobilization against the welfare state in the late 1970s. Lurid accounts in George Glider's *Wealth and Poverty* and Mickey Kaus's *The End of Equality* portrayed welfare and the poor as enemies of the democratic marketplace. President Ronald Reagan picked up these themes and contributed his own colorful anecdotes about welfare cheats and fraud, as he pushed forward cuts in taxes and social welfare programs. These forays into the politics of personal piety fit a Republican electoral strategy aimed at mobilizing the religious right and bringing the white working class into the party fold.

Out with the "Old" Welfare

Reforming welfare assumed new urgency in the 1990s, an urgency grounded less in policy realities than in electoral politics. Alarms were sounded about a crisis of cost, although for three decades, spending on AFDC amounted to less than 2 percent of the federal budget. The $16 billion the federal government allocated to AFDC was dwarfed by spending on Social Security and defense, each costing more than $300 billion per year. Public opinion polls, however, indicated a different perception. Forty percent of respondents believed that welfare was one of the most expensive national programs, even larger than Social Security or defense.

Polls also indicated that much of the public believed welfare recipients had it too easy, although few knew what welfare really provided. In fact, AFDC gave only meager support to poor families. In 1996, the median monthly benefit for a family of three was $366. Even when combined with food stamps, welfare lifted few poor families above the federal poverty line. Even the much-touted crisis of dependency ("dependent" being a term loosely applied to anyone receiving welfare) was not reflected in the evidence. The share of families receiving welfare for extended periods declined between 1970 and 1985 and leveled off after that. Families that received welfare for more than six years constituted only a small minority of the welfare caseload at any point in time.

Although the hue and cry over a supposed welfare crisis was greatly overblown, Bill Clinton clearly appreciated welfare's potent political symbolism. As a presidential candidate, he famously pledged to "end welfare as we know it," a turn of phrase useful in demonstrating that he was a "new Democrat" unburdened by the liberalism of his predecessors. His proposals for reform emphasized neoliberal themes of work and individual responsibility, but coupled demands for work with provision of social services intended to improve individual employment prospects. . . .

Enter the "New" Welfare

The Personal Responsibility and Work Opportunity Reconciliation Act of 1996 replaced AFDC with a program aptly named Temporary Assistance to Needy Families (TANF). AFDC had provided an open-ended entitlement of federal funds to states based on the amount of benefits they distributed to poor families. TANF ended that entitlement, establishing a five-year block grant fixed at $16.5 billion annually (based on the amount allocated to AFDC in its last year) that states could draw down to subsidize welfare and related expenditures.

Mistrusting the states' willingness to be tough enough on work, Congress incorporated detailed and coercive provisions. First, it set time limits for assistance, restricting federal aid to a lifetime maximum of sixty months. If states wanted to exceed those limits, they would have to pay for most of it themselves. Second, parents were required to work or participate in so-called work activities after a maximum of two years of welfare receipt. Third, TANF established escalating work quotas. States that wanted to collect their full portion of federal dollars would have to show, by 2002, that 50 percent of adults heading single-parent households were working thirty hours per week. Fourth, it meticulously specified those work

> *"Most states [have] made no effort to assure access to food stamps for those losing welfare."*

"activities" that would enable states to meet their quotas, among them paid work, job search, and unpaid workfare (in which recipients "worked off" their welfare benefits at minimum wage or provided child care for other welfare recipients). It limited the use of education and vocational training as countable activities.

> *"More than a fifth of those leaving welfare for work return within a year or two."*

Although the "work" side of TANF was clearly pre-eminent, there were some modest provisions on the "opportunity" side, with Congress providing $2.3 billion to help subsidize child care for working mothers and $3 billion in a block grant for welfare-to-work programs.

Beyond these prominent features, the new welfare also packed some hidden punches. It rewarded states for cutting welfare caseloads, largely without regard to how they did it. States that reduced their caseloads (whether those losing welfare found work or not) received credit against officially mandated quotas. If Congress was worried about states' slacking off from its tough work demands, the law indicated no concern that they might go too far in restricting access to benefits or pushing people off the welfare rolls. Only caseload reductions counted.

Under the banner of devolution, the law also gave states new authority to design their own welfare programs. While the welfare debate highlighted the professed virtues of innovation, less obvious was the license it gave states to craft policies even tougher and more restrictive than those allowed by federal law.

Pushing welfare decision making to the state and local level has never been good for the poor. In many states, poor families and their allies have little political influence. Moreover, constitutional balanced-budget requirements make states structurally unsuited to the task of protecting vulnerable residents against economic slumps. When unemployment goes up and state tax revenue goes down, the downward pressure on social spending intensifies.

The secret triumph of devolution lay, not in the opportunities for innovation, but in the opportunity for a quiet unraveling of the safety net.

The Unfolding Story of Welfare Transformed

What has happened since 1996? For one thing, the new welfare changed a national program of income assistance to an array of state programs, each with its own assortment of benefits, services, restrictions, and requirements. There has always been wide variation in the amount of cash aid states provided, and federal waivers allowed states to deviate from some national rules. But devolution spurred far greater policy inconsistency by allowing states, essentially, to make their own rules. Consequently, what you get (or whether you get anything at all) depends on where you live.

In addition, devolution set off a state "race to the bottom," not by reducing benefit levels as some had predicted, but by imposing new restrictions that limited access to benefits. States across the nation have taken advantage of devolution to impose restrictions tougher than those required by federal law.

For example, although federal law required recipients to work within two years, most states require work within one year, some require immediate work, and others demand a month of job search before they even begin to process an application for assistance. No longer required to exempt mothers with children under three years old from work requirements, most states permit an exemption only for mothers with babies under one year old, and some have eliminated exemptions altogether. In nineteen states, lifetime limits for welfare receipt are set below the federal maximum of sixty months. Other states have imposed so-called family caps that preclude benefits for babies born to mothers already receiving welfare. If federal policymakers secretly hoped that states would do part of the dirty work of cutting welfare for them, they must be pleased with these results. . . .

The picture becomes still more complicated when one attempts to peer behind the head count in order to assess what actually happened in the purge of welfare caseloads. Exactly how did states push those caseloads down? What has happened to poor families that no longer have recourse to welfare? What kind of opportunities does the lower wage labor market really offer? Research has only begun to illuminate these crucial questions, but the evidence is disheartening.

Beyond the Caseload Count

Finding good jobs: There are three ways to lower welfare caseloads. One is by successfully moving recipients into good jobs with stable employment where they can earn enough to maintain their families above poverty (or, at least, above what they could get on welfare). Recipients may find jobs on their own, which many do, or with connections facilitated by welfare agencies and service providers.

Financial supports provided by TANF have allowed some recipients to take jobs where they earn too little to make ends meet on their own. Child-care and transportation subsidies make a difference for those workers. They also benefit from federally funded food stamps that stretch the grocery budget. But food stamp use fell off 40 percent after 1994, although fewer families were receiving welfare and more had joined the ranks of the working poor.

> *"The family-friendly workplace . . . couldn't be farther from the hard reality of lower wage jobs."*

Absent external pressures, most states made no effort to assure access to food stamps for those losing welfare. In fact, government studies indicate that administrative hassles and misinformation discouraged low-income families from obtaining benefits.

Taking bad jobs: A second way to lower welfare caseloads is to pressure recipients into taking bad jobs. Not all lower wage jobs are bad, but many of those most readily available to former recipients undermine their best efforts to make it as working parents. These jobs are characterized by unstable schedules, limited access to health insurance or pensions, no sick leave, and job insecurity. Because high turnover is a feature of these jobs, at any given moment, many are apt to be available. Indeed, employers seeking to fill these undesirable "high-velocity" jobs, where there is continuous churning of the workforce, are all too eager to use welfare agencies as a hiring hall.

> *"Welfare . . . offers little leeway to acquire either the time or skills that might yield a job with a future."*

This may partially explain why more than a fifth of those leaving welfare for work return within a year or two. Proponents of the new welfare conveniently blame individual work behavior or attitudes for job churning, but ignore the role of employers who structure jobs in ways that make job loss inevitable. What's a supermarket clerk to do when her manager makes frequent schedule changes, periodically shortens her hours, or asks her to work in a store across town? What happens is that carefully constructed child care arrangements break down, lost pay days break the family budget, and the hours it takes to commute on public transportation become unmanageable. The family-friendly workplace that more sought-after workers demand couldn't be farther from the hard reality of lower wage jobs.

One of the little appreciated virtues of the old welfare is that it served as a sort of unemployment insurance for these lower wage workers excluded from regular unemployment insurance by their irregular jobs. Welfare cushioned the layoffs, turnover, and contingencies that go with the territory. Under the new welfare, these workers face a hard landing because welfare is more difficult to get and offers little leeway to acquire either the time or skills that might yield a job with a future. Over the longer term, low-wage workers may find their access to welfare blocked by time limits. Although the five-year lifetime limit ostensibly targets sustained reliance on welfare, this limit could come back to bite those who cycle in and out of the lower wage labor force. At this point, no one knows how this will play out.

Benefits Are Harder to Acquire

Creating barriers to access: A third way to reduce welfare caseloads is by reducing access—making benefits harder to acquire and keep. Some states explicitly try to divert applicants by imposing advance job-search requirements, demanding multiple trips to the welfare office in order to complete the application process, or informally advising applicants that it may not be worth the hassle. In some welfare offices, caseworkers routinely encourage applicants to forgo cash aid and apply only for Medicaid and food stamps.

Benefits are also harder to keep, as caseworkers require recipients to attend frequent meetings either to discuss seemingly endless demands for documentation or to press them on issues involving work. Everyday life in an urban welfare office is difficult to describe and, for many, even harder to believe. There are the hours of waiting in rows of plastic chairs, the repeated requests for paperwork, the ritualized weekly job club lectures about how to smile, shake hands, and show a good attitude to employers. As inspiration, caseworkers leading job club sessions often tell stories from their own lives of rising from poverty to become welfare workers (positions likely to be cut back as caseloads decline). When clients tell their own tales of cycling from bad jobs to worse and ask for help getting a good job, caseworkers are apt to admonish them for indulging in a "pity party."

Access to welfare may also be constrained through a profoundly mundane array of administrative barriers that simply make benefits harder to keep. A missed appointment, misplaced documents (often lost by the agency), delayed entry of personal data—these common and otherwise trivial mishaps can result in a loss of benefits for "non-cooperation."

The Public Benefits Hotline,[1] a call-in center that provides both advice and intervention for Chicago residents, received some ten thousand calls in the four years after welfare reform, most of them involving hassles of this sort. In other parts of the country, these types of problems show up in

> **"Most big cities have been reporting worrisome increases in homelessness and hunger."**

administrative hearing records and court cases, where judges have criticized welfare agencies for making "excessive" demands for verification documents, conducting "sham assessments" leading to inappropriate imposition of work requirements, and sanctioning clients for missing appointments when they should have helped them deal with child care or medical difficulties.

Is There a Bottom Line?

The new welfare has produced neither the immediate cataclysm its opponents threatened nor the economic and social redemption its proponents anticipated. Opponents had warned that welfare reform would plunge one million children into poverty. In the midst of an unprecedented economic boom, that didn't happen. But, even in the best of times, prospects were not auspicious for those leaving welfare.

According to the Urban Institute, about half of those leaving welfare for work between 1997 and 1999 obtained jobs where they earned a median hourly wage of only $7.15. If the jobs offered a steady forty hours of work a week (which

---

1. The hotline is a collaborative effort of the Legal Assistance Foundation of Chicago and community antipoverty advocates.

lower wage jobs usually don't), that would provide a gross annual income of $14,872. That places a mother with two children a precarious $1,000 above the formal poverty line for the year 2000 and a two-parent family with two children nearly $3,000 *below* that line. But more than one-fifth of those leaving welfare for work didn't make it through the year—either because they lost their jobs, got sick, or just couldn't make ends meet. The only thing surprising about these

> **"Inequality is growing and poverty is deepening."**

figures is that the numbers weren't higher. Others left or lost welfare, but did not find work, with one in seven adults losing welfare reporting no alternative means of support. Their specific fate is unknown, but most big cities have been reporting worrisome increases in homelessness and hunger.

If there is any bottom line, it is that caseloads have been purged. But neither the market for lower wage workers nor the policies put into practice in the name of welfare reform have purged poverty from the lives of the poor. Even in the last years of the economic boom, between 1996 and 1998, the Urban Institute found that three hundred thousand more individuals in single-parent families slipped into extreme poverty. Although they qualified for food stamps that might have stretched their resources a bit further, many did not get them. Government figures indicate that families leaving welfare for work often lose access to other benefits, which states do not automatically continue irrespective of eligibility.

More recently, census figures have begun to show the effects of recession coupled with an eroded safety net. The nation's poverty rate rose to 11.7 percent in 2001, up from 11.3 percent the prior year. More troubling still, inequality is growing and poverty is deepening. In 2001, the "poverty gap," the gap between the official poverty line and the income of poor individuals, reached its highest level since measurements were first taken in 1979. In California, often a harbinger of larger social trends, a startling two in three poor children now live in families where at least one adult is employed. Can the families of lower wage workers live without access to welfare and other government supports? Apparently, they can live, but not very well. . . .

Welfare, though small in scope, is large in relevance because it is a place where economic, social, and political issues converge. The old welfare acknowledged, in principle, a political commitment to relieve poverty and lessen inequality, even if, in practice, that commitment was limited, benefits were ungenerous, and access uneven. The new welfare dramatically changed the terms of the relationship between disadvantaged citizens and their state. It devolved choices about social protection from the State to the states, and it placed the value of work over the values of family well-being and social equity. As bad as the old welfare may have been, there is reason to lament its demise after all.

Welfare Reform Has Not Reduced Poverty

by Angie O'Gorman

About the author: *Angie O'Gorman is a freelance writer and researcher living in St. Louis, Missouri. She is also the director of the Immigration Law Project at Legal Services of Eastern Missouri.*

Welfare, at least as we have known it [since 1996] expires on Sept. 30, 2002. The reauthorization process is well under way and will set the direction for social and family policy for the foreseeable future.[1] It seems a suitable time, therefore, to evaluate the 1996 reform—"the first significant conservative welfare policy of the postwar period," according to Robert Rector, senior research fellow with the Heritage Foundation. How did it do, for example, in terms of reducing poverty? A reasonable question. But not a fair one, according to the supporters of welfare reform.

This not a fair question because poverty reduction was not a statutory goal of welfare reform. The primary goal was to reduce the number of people dependent on government support in lieu of employment. Many Americans assumed, from the resulting emphasis on self-sufficiency through employment, that wages were the way out of poverty. They were wrong.

Many also still think that poverty reduction should be the benchmark for assessing the reform's success. In a national survey recently released by the Packard Foundation, 74 percent of respondents said that decreasing the number of families in poverty should be very important in judging welfare reform. "The public agrees," states the report, "that improving conditions for families and children should be an important part of assessing the success of welfare reform."

But there is little agreement about the existence of poverty in the United States to begin with, let alone its cause and meaning. The Heritage Foundation,

---

1. Congress extended the benefits provided by the 1996 Welfare Reform Law until a reauthorized welfare bill could be passed.

for example, argues that poverty does not exist to the extent believed and claims that it is just the result of how the government processes the numbers. Mr. Rector finds that America's "poor" suffer from behavioral rather than fiscal deficits. "The culture of the underclass," he stated in an essay in 2000 titled "Broadening the Reform," "is remarked by a cluster of behavioral pathologies, eroded work ethic, collapse of marriage, indifference to education, drug and alcohol abuse, and pervasive crime." Offering a different perspective, Network, a national Catholic social justice lobby, notes the following in its own report, *Welfare Reform: How Do We Define Success:* "The long-term health of the U.S. economic system depends on whether the basic needs of all people in the country are met. Until and unless this nation attends to the needs of people who do not benefit from economic progress, millions of people in the U.S. will continue to live in poverty."

Those who hold the poor-as-pathological view to one degree or another see welfare itself as the problem. They assert that these social pathologies would not exist if it were not for the welfare policies established since Lyndon B. Johnson first declared war on poverty in 1964. They are partially correct.

Welfare as We Knew It

Under the old system, the rules of eligibility barred recipients (usually mothers and children) from working or from marrying an employed male. If a mother did either of these, she lost her welfare check. Period. Working and receiving welfare at the same time was cheating, breaking the law, fraud. Interestingly enough, Mr. Rector's own studies show that over one-third of welfare fraud under the old system was illegal employment—thereby casting doubt on his view that pathological laziness causes poverty. The general pattern under the old system was for recipient to receive welfare for a few years, leave and then return after a few more years, because they were unable to find a steady economic footing. There was a clear cycle of moving on and off the rolls.

Few would disagree that this system had a degenerative effect on recipients—many argued that opinion throughout its 42-year run. The cause of those effects, however, continues as a matter of debate. Was it because welfare fed the poor's pathological tendencies, or because the system trapped recipients into life at a subsistence level in the midst of surrounding wealth? Was it the poor who were pathological, or poverty, or the system itself?

> *"Welfare reform, as embodied in the Temporary Aid to Needy Families program . . . , included severely punitive measures."*

Personal, not social, responsibility was the reform cry in 1996 that yielded the Personal Responsibility and Work Opportunity Act of 1996. The act was based on assumptions of laziness, sloth, malintent and a tendency among the poor to cheat. The poor-as-pathological stance had become public policy. While the surrounding debate acknowledged the prior system's structural bar to self-sufficiency, it blamed recipients for poverty in the United States. Thus welfare reform, as embodied in the Temporary Aid to Needy Families program (TANF), included severely punitive measures like full-family sanctions (termination of cash assistance because a parent violated a requirement), rigid time limits even if recipients were employed but poor and limits on education and training.

> *"As more single mothers went to work, there was an increase in child neglect."*

Past welfare restrictions, racism, lack of a livable wage, downsizing, unstable employment, lack of access to equal justice, inadequate health care and housing were not acknowledged as objective causes of poverty. Poverty was seen as a matter of personal pathology, one that responded best to punitive measures. Thus caseload reduction became the goal. In short, having demonized welfare recipients as pathological parasites, the law focused on getting them off our national, tax-paying back. This we have largely accomplished.

Are Children Better Off?

According to Wade Horn, assistant secretary of health and human services, the right question to ask of welfare reform is: "Are children better off?" Mr. Rector, a proponent of a yes response to this question, points out that "the decline in welfare dependence has been greatest among the most disadvantaged and least employable single mothers—the group with the greatest tendency toward long-term dependence." He sees in this a confirmation that welfare reform affected the entire welfare caseload, not merely the most employable mothers. And one could reasonably conclude that if the children of the most disadvantaged are better off, surely the children of the less disadvantaged are that much more so.

What this logic fails to note is that participation in TANF assistance fell much more rapidly than did poverty, partly because of the states' use of full-family sanctions. Indeed, it was precisely the group mentioned by Mr. Rector who were the most sanctioned. Significant also is the fact that the majority of people leaving TANF for employment entered low-wage jobs and continue there.

The typical "leaver," someone previously on TANF, is a single woman with two children. She is working full time at minimum wage and receives $10,300 in wages annually, or $178 per week. The poverty level for a family of three is currently $14,600. The government subsidizes her employer by making up the difference between her wage and a livable wage through food stamps. Medicaid, CHIP (Children's Health Insurance Program) and other government benefits. One could reasonably wonder why taxpayers are subsidizing business in this manner.

While caseloads fell by roughly 50 percent between 1995 and 2000, the number of children in poverty fell 22 percent. As noted in a study by the Center for

Law and Social Policy in January 2002, "In 1994, 62 percent of poor children were receiving assistance through Aid to Families with Dependent Children; by 1999 only 40 percent of poor children were receiving TANF assistance." There were not fewer poor children, only fewer of them receiving assistance. There is no essential connection between a family leaving TANF and a family leaving poverty. Many of those least employable mothers mentioned by Rector remain just that, least employable, but now without assistance.

Increased Employment Is Not Enough

What is the relationship between the drop in caseloads and the goal set out by Mr. Horn? At the moment that is an unanswerable question. It is simply not clear how TANF has affected children. There are, however, studies of pre-TANF programs in states whose welfare reform experiments were later incorporated into the federal model. Two findings are of particular interest in relation to Mr. Horn's question.

First, TANF's positive effects depend on improved income, not just increased employment. Without increased income, the academic achievement and behavior of young and adolescent children were negatively affected. TANF programs that led to increased earnings but not increased incomes—because benefits losses offset earnings gains—showed no clear positive effect on children. In other words, increased employment alone is not sufficient to foster healthy development of children. Increased income is the key. Second,

> *"[Sixty] percent of employed [welfare] leavers are living at or below the poverty level—the majority in jobs that do not carry health insurance."*

red flags were raised by these studies regarding the impact of TANF-type policies on rates of child maltreatment, particularly neglect.

Between 1995 and 1999, the estimated number of children in foster care grew from 483,000 to 568,000, an increase of 85,000. Regarding Mr. Rector's comment about the most disadvantaged leavers, it is important to note that as more single mothers went to work, there was an increase in child neglect, a pattern concentrated among the most disadvantaged—those with the fewest resources to overcome the combined effect of low-wage work and welfare loss. Studies to date show a trend indicating that TANF grant reductions increased entries into the child welfare system, a phenomenon strongest among families who had been sanctioned. Trends also showed an increased delay in family reunification, because mothers were overwhelmed by the stress of poverty coupled with welfare requirements. Employed mothers who experienced TANF grant reductions were reunified with their children nine times more slowly than other mothers. In short, the loss of benefits combined with low-wage employment appears to increase neglect. . . .

One would not be completely out in left field if one wondered whether the real agenda of the 1996 reform was to create and sustain a pool of low-wage labor. How else can we call the reform a success when 60 percent of employed leavers are living at or below the poverty level—the majority in jobs that do not carry health insurance? In 1999, 59 percent of single mothers in families with incomes below 200 percent of the poverty level were working. And studies that track leavers over longer periods show no significant earnings growth after leaving welfare. In 1999, amid a blooming economy, the poorest 700,000 single mothers living only with their children had lower earned income than similar women in 1985, even though their earnings increased. In other words, the lowest-income single mothers had become poorer.

A review of current conservative literature on welfare and its reform shows literally no mention of the term "salary" or its equivalents: "wage," "fair wage," "living wage" or "sustainable wage." It is the missing link in welfare reform, just as poverty reduction was the missing goal. While President [George W.] Bush's reauthorization proposal, "Working Toward Independence," would increase the number of required work hours per week for TANF recipients, it is silent on the issue of a living wage. But to clarify the administration's concern about wages, Tommy G. Thompson, secretary of health and human services, stated on March 6, 2002: "This administration recognizes that the only way to escape poverty is through work, and that is why we have made work and jobs that will pay at least the minimum wage the centerpiece of the reauthorization proposal . . . ."

"At least the minimum wage," as we have seen, does not raise a family out of poverty, no matter how hard a mother works.

That same day, the *Los Angeles Times* reported that President Bush was "moving to allow states to place welfare recipients in jobs that pay less than minimum wage," as a form of "supervised work experience." Replacing the term "employment" with that of "supervised work experience" removes the recipient from any minimum-wage requirement and labor protections. And this is the plan for those with the greatest barriers to employment, such as mental, physical or emotional handicaps, care for a disabled or sick family member, child care, lack of transportation and other drawbacks to independence. Yet the Bush proposal does not give states adequate flexibility in terms of counting education and training as work activity, thus lessening the already inadequate attention to these factors needed to obtain a job that pays a living wage.

One escapes poverty by hard work that pays a livable wage. The number of families that have left welfare since 1996 is 2.3 million. But most have yet to leave poverty. Is it not time to turn our attention to making work pay, so that poverty drops as well as the caseloads? When you think about it, the only fair question is, how has the 1996 reform done at reducing poverty?

Welfare Reform Will Add to the Ranks of the Homeless

by Paul Freese Jr. and Sacha Klein-Martin

About the authors: *Paul Freese Jr. is director of litigation and advocacy at Public Counsel Law Center in Los Angeles, California. Sacha Klein-Martin is a social work intern researching the impact of welfare reform.*

As you ponder the likely consequences of the proposed [2003] state budget cuts [in California], take a drive through skid row. Witness the Third World country growing right in our midst. Note in particular the influx of homeless families that is overwhelming emergency shelter resources there, with their young children spilling into the street to play amidst dope pushers, prostitutes, dirty needles, and parolees.

Many of these families are the early casualties of welfare reform, yet they are a modest precursor of what's to come as [Los Angeles] county braces for the impact of 5-year time limits reducing welfare checks for thousands of families who are barely able to make rent as it is.

State budget cuts threaten dramatically to reduce welfare to work programs and child care support that these families desperately need to find employment to replace the income they are about to lose—all in the midst of a faltering national economy.

A Homeless Explosion

In early 1998 Los Angeles confronted a similar phenomenon—the first historic imposition of time limits on the welfare program of last resort for single adults known as General Relief [GR]. In 1997, Public Counsel warned in an op-ed for the *Business Journal* that cutting GR risked precipitating a "homeless explosion" because of the number of individuals who relied upon GR to keep themselves housed in Single Room Occupancy units.

It is painful to witness what we feared come to pass—to the point that L.A. now has the largest and most unmanageable homeless population on skid row ever. Now we are at an even more critical juncture with welfare reform about to cut benefits for thousands of L.A. County families that could generate sprawling numbers of homeless families.

The theory behind the GR time limits was no different than what's behind impending cuts to welfare for families (known as CAL-WORKS). Both assume that these cuts should create an incentive for the affected individuals to more aggressively pursue work opportunities.

The problem with this theory is that those affected are chronically unemployable and underemployed for reasons often beyond their control. Most are single women who desperately need childcare, but find themselves on the county's long waiting lists for such assistance. More than one third of these individuals suffer from a severe mental health problem that interferes with their ability to get or keep a job, according to the General Accounting Office.

> *"Homelessness increases the odds that parents will become chronically unemployed and abandon hope of living a normal life."*

Between 25 percent and 57 percent of women on welfare have symptoms of severe depression, such as chronic lethargy, confusion, despondency, and irritability—traits too often disparaged by welfare caseworkers and employers as character defects rather than illness. Many of these women are also fleeing domestic violence. The Taylor Institute reports that 30 percent of women on welfare were victims of domestic violence within the past year.

Do such problems mean these individuals are unable to work? Of course not, as they'll be the first to tell you. But without help overcoming these problems, welfare recipients are not likely to find a steady job in L.A.'s competitive job market. The welfare cuts are certain to push families barely making it on their current welfare check ($679 month for a family of three) toward evictions and homelessness.

Survival Strategies

Once homeless, their children's education is disrupted, as are ties to friends and relatives. Summing up the dehumanizing experiences of moving for three years from shelter to shelter, an 11-year-old girl said desolately, "I died three years ago." Such childhood experiences of homelessness dramatically increase one's likelihood of becoming homeless as an adult, according to an extensive Rand study.

Homelessness increases the odds that parents will become chronically unemployed and abandon hope of living a normal life as contributing taxpayers. The lack of shelter itself becomes a major barrier to employment.

If children become endangered because they are living on the streets, Child Protective Services must take custody of them at a cost to taxpayers of $2,000 to $15,000 per month per child. While none of us relish the idea of raising taxes, the alternative is to reap these severe long-term economic costs downstream—not to mention the costs to our collective welfare, and conscience too, as a society seeking to be just.

Chapter 4

What Strategies Would Benefit the Poor and the Homeless?

Chapter Preface

Economists and poverty analysts have widely varying opinions on how to deal with poverty and homelessness in the United States. While some advocate a redistribution of wealth through taxation, charitable donations, government programs, or wage increases, others maintain that the poor benefit more from an expanding free market economy that increases profits for business and industry.

Those who champion economic growth as a means to address poverty often argue that the income gap between the rich and the poor is normal in a capitalist society. A free market economy, they contend, encourages entrepreneurship and upward mobility. However, it also presupposes that those whose skills are in demand command higher incomes while less-skilled workers generally earn less. Thus, income levels naturally vary according to workers' skill levels and societal needs. In the opinion of W. Michael Cox and Richard Alm, authors of *Myths of Rich and Poor*, such income disparity is not a form of social inequity, because the poor have opportunities to improve their lot: "America isn't a caste society, and studies that track individuals' income over time show that Americans have a remarkable ability to propel themselves forward." Statistics support this claim. According to a study of lifetime earnings by the Federal Reserve Bank of Dallas, only 5 percent of people in the economy's lowest 20 percent fail to move into a higher income group. In other words, if the poor are willing to work and develop needed skills, most of them do not remain poor. Moreover, argue Cox and Alm, policies that attempt to eliminate wealth gaps—such as higher taxation or wage increases—often do more harm than good: "Higher taxation might narrow the division between rich and poor, but it would be a hollow triumph if it stifled the economy. What Americans ought to care most about is maintaining our growth, not the red herring of gaps in income and wealth."

But other analysts maintain that economists like Cox and Alm have succumbed to a cultural myth about the poor: the notion that poverty is inevitable. According to activist and author Jim Tull, this belief in the inevitability of poverty actually helps to sustain it. "I find this myth [about poverty] debilitating," says Tull. "It has convinced us that there is no sense in trying to end poverty; that the best we can hope for is to lessen it. And it has blinded us to how poverty, far from being the fate of humanity, is the product of the way we have structured our civilization." Anthropologists who agree with Tull often point out that hunter-gatherer peoples, who lived for hundreds of thousands of years before modern civilization, equitably distributed resources and freely shared in the care of others in mutually supportive networks. The scattered pockets of tribal people who still live this way are, in Tull's opinion, "living proof that poverty is a function of culture, not of nature." Tull maintains that while modern people genuinely desire to help the needy, they often lack the time or the opportunities to do so. It may even be that "we cling to the continuation of poverty because we need a place to express our frustrated inclination toward compassion," states Tull.

Some experts see signs that a growing number of people are openly challenging the idea that poverty is inevitable. According to organizer and editor Jim Wallis, a new generation of activists, inspired by the twentieth-century civil rights movement, has begun to build a values-based political reform movement that is unapologetic about the need for economic justice. "Many voices are now calling for a renewed commitment to the common good over the bottom line, and an ethic of both personal and social responsibility. Many are finding that engagement in their communities provides practical solutions toward overcoming poverty," Wallis asserts. Such solutions include building grassroots coalitions between labor unions, neighborhood activists, charitable organizations, and businesses as well as supporting local efforts to increase poor people's access to job training, livable wages, child care, public transportation, and affordable housing.

In the following chapter, several authors discuss in greater detail the problem of how to help the poor and the homeless. Their suggestions—from encouraging marriage for single mothers to giving spare change to the homeless—offer a variety of perspectives on society's role in confronting poverty.

Promoting Marriage Would Reduce Poverty

by Robert E. Rector, Kirk A. Johnson, Patrick F. Fagan, and Lauren R. Noyes

About the authors: *Robert E. Rector is Senior Research Fellow, Kirk A. John-son is Harry and Jeanette Weinberg Fellow in Statistical Welfare Research in the Center for Data Analysis, Patrick F. Fagan is William H.G. Fitzgerald Re-search Fellow in Family and Cultural Issues, and Lauren R. Noyes is director of research projects at the Heritage Foundation.*

In 2001, 1.35 million children were born outside marriage. This represents 33.5 percent of all children born in the United States in that year. Children raised by never-married mothers are seven times more likely to be poor when compared to children raised in intact married families. The obvious nexus between single-parent families and child poverty has led President George W. Bush to propose a new trial program aimed at increasing child well-being and reducing child poverty by promoting healthy marriage.[1]

Critics have rejected President Bush's proposal as illogical. They argue that increasing marriage would not significantly reduce child poverty for two reasons: first, that there is a substantial shortage of suitable males for single mothers to marry, and second, that even if single mothers married the father of their children, the earnings of the fathers are so low that they would not lift the family out of poverty.

The Fragile Families Study

However, new light has been shed on the status of non-married parents through the recent Fragile Families and Child Well-Being Study. The Fragile Families survey is a nation-wide effort to collect data on both married and non-married parents at the time of a child's birth. The survey reveals that most of

---

1. As this volume went to press, this program had not been enacted.

the claims about marriage and non-married fathers made by the opponents of the Bush "healthy marriage" proposal are wildly inaccurate.

The Fragile Families Study shows the following:

• The median age of non-married mothers is 22 at the time of birth of the child.

• Nearly three-quarters of non-married mothers are in a relatively stable romantic relationship with the expectant father at around the time of birth of their child.

• The expectant non-married fathers who have a romantic involvement with the mother-to-be are quite "marriageable." Very few have drug, alcohol, or physical abuse problems.

> *"In the overwhelming majority of cases, marriage would lift families out of poverty."*

• On average, the earnings of non-married expectant fathers are higher than the earnings of expectant mothers in the year before the child's birth.

• The median annual earnings of non-married fathers are approximately $17,500 per year.

In this *CDA Report*,[2] the Fragile Families data are used to calculate how much marriage could reduce poverty among couples who are not married at the time of the child's birth. This analysis finds that marriage would dramatically reduce poverty among the non-married mothers who are romantically involved with the fathers at the time of the child's birth.

Specifically, if these mothers do not marry but remain single, about 55 percent will be poor. By contrast, if all the mothers married their child's father, the poverty rate would fall to less than 17 percent. Thus, on average, marriage would reduce the odds that a mother and a child will live in poverty by more than 70 percent.

The contention, made by critics of the President's marriage-strengthening policy, that increased marriage will not reduce child poverty because fathers do not earn enough to lift a family out of poverty is inaccurate. While marriage of mothers and fathers would not eliminate child poverty in every case, in the overwhelming majority of cases, marriage would lift families out of poverty. Overall, the insights culled from the Fragile Families dataset and described in this *CDA Report* strongly indicate that a policy aimed at promoting healthy marriage among young parents has enormous potential to reduce child poverty. . . .

Characteristics of Non-Married Parents

Some 38 percent of the mothers in the Fragile Families Study were not married at the time of their child's birth. Popular opinion sees out-of-wedlock childbearing as occurring mainly to young girls of high-school age who lack stable relationships with their child's father. This perception is erroneous. The

---

2. CDA is an acronym for Center for Data Analysis, a group within the Heritage Foundation that provides research and data for policy makers.

median age for mothers who give birth outside marriage is 22.

Nor are non-married mothers alone and isolated at the time of birth. As [research] shows, nearly 50 percent of these mothers are cohabiting with the expectant father at around the time of the child's birth. Another 23 percent describe themselves as "romantically involved" with the father, although the couple is not cohabiting.

The characteristics of non-married fathers who are cohabiting or romantically involved with the mother are generally more favorable than the popular stereotype. Around 67 percent of the fathers have at least a high-school degree. Some 97 percent were employed during the prior year, and 82 percent were employed at the time of the child's birth. The median annual income of these romantically involved/cohabiting fathers was between $15,000 and $20,000.

Among romantically involved or cohabiting couples, physical abuse is rare: A full 98 percent of the women in this group report that the father has never slapped them when angry. While some fathers do have drug and alcohol problems, the level is less than might be expected: Around 12 percent of the mothers report arguing with their boyfriends about a drug or alcohol problem in the last month; 2.5 percent report that drugs or alcohol impede the boyfriend's ability to hold a job.

> *"A policy aimed at promoting healthy marriage . . . has enormous potential to reduce child poverty."*

On average, the non-married expectant fathers have higher earnings than the expectant mothers in the year before the child's birth. The median wage rate of fathers is $8.55 per hour, compared to $7.00 per hour for the mothers.

Nearly all couples that are romantically involved or cohabiting are interested in developing a long-term, stable relationship. Some 95 percent believe that there is at least a 50/50 chance they will marry in the future.

Marriage Simulation

The purpose of this *CDA Report* is to calculate the reduction in poverty that would occur if non-married women married the fathers of their new children around the time of the child's birth. As [research shows], some non-married pregnant women [27 percent] do not have positive and stable relationships with their child's father. In these cases, marriage is not, for the most part, a reasonable option. Therefore, we have restricted our initial marriage simulation to the 73 percent of non-married couples who were cohabiting or romantically involved but living apart at the time of their child's birth. We shall henceforth refer to these couples as the "marriageable group."

To determine the impact of marriage on the poverty of children and mothers, we first estimate what the poverty rate of the mothers would be if they remained single. We then calculate what the poverty rate would be if the mother and father marry. The difference between the poverty rate of the mothers when single and the rate for mothers when married demonstrates the potential for marriage to reduce child poverty and maternal poverty.

• *Employment and Earnings.* The Fragile Families survey contains data on the annual earnings of new fathers in the year before the child was born. We employ these annual earnings figures in our analysis. The study also provides annual earnings for

> *"Marriage combined with part-time maternal employment . . . raises nearly all families above poverty."*

mothers in the year before birth. However, women's participation in the labor force may be altered significantly by the birth of a child. Because of this, the paper estimates mothers' post-birth earnings based on a range of assumptions concerning future hours of employment.

Specifically, we have calculated the effect of marriage on poverty according to three separate scenarios relating to the mothers' employment after the child's birth.

• *Scenario No. 1:* The mother has zero annual employment after the birth.
• *Scenario No. 2:* The mother is employed part-time for a total of 1,000 hours per year after the birth.
• *Scenario No. 3:* The mother is employed full-time throughout the year after the birth for a total of 2,000 hours.

In each scenario, the annual earnings of the fathers are assumed to be the same as the earnings in the year before the child's birth. The annual earnings of the mother are derived by multiplying the mother's hourly wage rate by the specified hours worked. In each scenario, the employment and earnings of a mother are assumed to be unchanged by marriage; that is, the mother is assumed to earn the same amount when married as when single.

• *Welfare Benefits.* The simulation assumes that single mothers will be eligible for TANF (Temporary Assistance for Needy Families), EITC (Earned Income Tax Credit), and food stamps. The level of benefits that a single mother would receive from each program is determined by the number of children in the family and the mother's annual earnings. Simulations for married couples assume that they are eligible only for food stamps and the EITC. The couple's earnings and family size determine the value of benefits. It is assumed that no married couples will receive TANF benefits.

The Effect of Marriage on Poverty

Under each scenario, we calculate the percentage of mothers who would be poor if they lived as single parents and the percentage who would be poor if they were married to the child's father.

• *Scenario No. 1: The mother is unemployed.* Chart 1 shows the impact of marriage on maternal and child poverty under Scenario No. 1. In this scenario, the

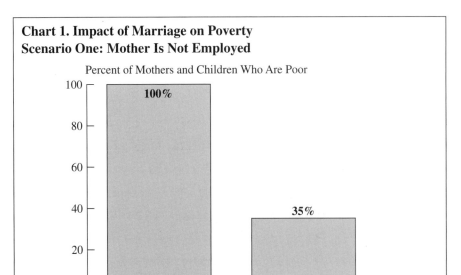

Chart 1. Impact of Marriage on Poverty
Scenario One: Mother Is Not Employed

Percent of Mothers and Children Who Are Poor

Source: Fragile Families and Child Well-Being Study.

mothers are not employed after the birth of the child. When single, the mothers are solely dependent on welfare (TANF and food stamps). When married, the mothers are solely dependent on the father's earnings plus EITC and food stamps.

As Chart 1 shows, if mothers remain single and unemployed, they will be poor 100 percent of the time. This is because welfare benefits alone rarely, if ever, provide enough income to raise a family above the poverty level. By contrast, if the mother marries the child's father, the poverty rate drops dramatically to 35 percent. In other words, nearly two-thirds of the non-married fathers within the marriageable group earn enough by themselves to support a family above poverty without any employment on the part of the mother.

Under the conditions of Scenario No. 1, marriage more than doubles the family income of mothers and children. If unmarried, the mothers would have a median income of around $8,800. Marriage would raise the mothers' median family income by over $11,000 to $20,226.

> *"Marriage would raise the family incomes of many full-time working mothers . . . into middle-class levels."*

• *Scenario No. 2: The mother is employed part-time.* Chart 2 shows the impact of marriage on child poverty under Scenario No. 2. In this scenario, mothers are assumed to be employed part-time for a total of 1,000 hours per year after the birth of their child. This scenario closely matches the employment rates

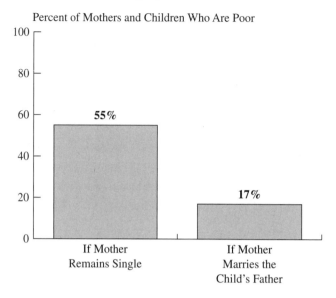

Chart 2. Impact of Marriage on Poverty
Scenario Two: Mother Is Employed Part-Time*

Percent of Mothers and Children Who Are Poor

*Note: Part-time employment means the mother is employed 1,000 hours per year whether single or married.
Source: Fragile Families and Child Well-Being Study.

of single mothers with young children as reported by the U.S. Bureau of the Census. Thus, it is the most realistic of the three scenarios.

Single mothers are assumed to receive income from earnings, EITC, food stamps, and, in some cases, TANF. Married couples are assumed to receive income from earnings, EITC, and food stamps. In this scenario, mothers are assumed to work 1,000 hours per year, whether single or married.

As Chart 2 shows, 55 percent of the mothers in the Fragile Families Study will live in poverty if they remain single and are employed part-time. By contrast, if the mothers marry, their poverty rate plummets to 17 percent. In other words, the father's normal earnings, combined with the part-time earnings of the mother, are sufficient to raise 83 percent of the families above the poverty line.

Under conditions of part-time maternal employment in Scenario No. 2, marriage increases family income by 75 percent. If unmarried, mothers would have a median income of around $13,500. Marriage would raise the mothers' median family income by around $10,000 to a level of $23,700.

Marriage combined with part-time maternal employment not only raises nearly all families above poverty, but in many cases also raises family income well above the poverty level. For example, under Scenario No. 2, less than 4 percent of single mothers would have family incomes above 150 percent of the poverty level. By contrast, about 46 percent of married couples would have an income above 150 percent of the poverty level.

• *Scenario No. 3: The mother is employed full-time.* Full-time/full-year employment is very effective in reducing poverty among single mothers. Some 90 percent of single mothers could maintain their families above poverty if they worked full-time throughout the year. (Full-time/full-year employment is equivalent to 2,000 annual hours of employment or 40 hours per week for 50 weeks.) Census Bureau data reveal that approximately 30 percent of single mothers with children under four are employed 2,000 hours or more per year.

Since very few single mothers who were employed full-time/full-year would remain poor, marriage has little effect in reducing poverty in this scenario. (Nearly 96 percent of married couples would have incomes above the poverty level, compared to 90 percent of single mothers.) However, marriage would raise the family incomes of many full-time working mothers well above poverty and into middle-class levels.

Full-time working mothers would have a median income of around $17,500 per year. If these mothers married their child's father, median family income would rise to $29,000 per year. . . . Nearly two-thirds of these married couples would have incomes above 150 percent of the poverty level. By contrast, only 20 percent of full-time working single mothers would have incomes above that level. . . .

A Pro-Marriage Initiative

Each year, more than 1.3 million children in the United States are born outside marriage. This represents 33.5 percent of all births. The Fragile Family survey shows that in 73 percent of out-of-wedlock births, the mother and father are romantically involved and have a relatively stable relationship.

Nearly half of non-married expectant mothers are cohabiting with the father at around the time of their child's birth. Overall, some 95 percent of non-married mothers express positive attitudes about marrying their new baby's father in the future. Yet only 9 percent of couples will actually marry within a year after their child's birth. Within a few years, the relationships of most of the non-married parents will deteriorate and the mother and father will split up.

As a new strategy for reducing child poverty and improving child well-being, President George W. Bush has proposed a new pilot program to promote healthy marriage. A principal target population of the President's proposed program would be romantically involved non-married couples at

> *"Marriage would eliminate poverty for the majority of poor single mothers."*

or around the "magic moment" of a child's birth. This target group is the precise population analyzed in this *CDA Report.*

Participation in the President's marriage program would be voluntary. The program would seek to increase healthy marriage by providing target couples with:

- Accurate information on the value of marriage in the lives of men, women, and children;
- Marriage-skills education that will enable couples to reduce conflict and increase the happiness and longevity of their relationship; and
- Experimental reductions in the current financial penalties against marriage that are contained in all federal welfare programs.

The programs would utilize existing marriage-skills education programs that have proven effective in decreasing conflict and increasing happiness and stability among couples. The pro-marriage initiative would not seek merely to increase marriage rates among target couples, but would provide ongoing support to help at-risk couples maintain healthy marriages over the long term.

"Over 80 percent of long-term child poverty occurs in broken or never-married families."

The President proposes to spend $300 million per year on his pilot program to promote healthy marriage. This modest sum represents spending only one cent to promote healthy marriage for every five dollars the government currently spends subsidizing single-parent families.

Critics of President Bush's proposal have charged that increasing the number of healthy marriages would not reduce child and maternal poverty. These claims are false and misleading.

For example, in a widely publicized paper entitled "Let Them Eat Wedding Rings: The Role of Marriage Promotion in Welfare Reform," an organization called Alternatives to Marriage asserted that "Marriage is not an effective solution to poverty." In fact, the actual study cited in the paper shows the opposite: Marriage would eliminate poverty for the majority of poor single mothers surveyed. Nevertheless, Alternatives to Marriage argues that marriage is not "an effective solution to poverty" because marriage would not eliminate poverty in *every* instance. The error of such an argument needs no further elaboration.

The analysis presented in this paper shows that marriage has an enormous potential to reduce poverty among couples who are unmarried at the time of their child's birth. In general, a 10 percent increase in the marriage rate of poor single mothers would reduce poverty among that group by 7 percentage points.

Increasing the number of healthy marriages would also have substantial non-economic benefits for children. Children who are raised in marriage by their biological mother and father are dramatically less likely to have emotional and behavioral problems, to be physically abused, to become involved in crime, to fail in school, to abuse drugs, and to end up on welfare as adults.

Healthy Marriage Is Critical

The erosion of marriage and the increase in single-parent families are major causes of child poverty and welfare dependence in the United States. Nearly three-quarters of government means-tested welfare aid to children goes to single-parent families. Over 80 percent of long-term child poverty occurs in broken or never-married families.

There is a widespread misconception that single mothers have little contact with the fathers of their children. In reality, surveys show that most non-married expectant mothers are romantically involved with their child's father at around the time of the child's birth. Most of these couples express positive attitudes about marriage and hope to become married in the future. Yet relatively few will, in fact, marry. Most will split apart a few years after the child's birth.

President George W. Bush has proposed a pilot program aimed at promoting healthy marriage, especially in low-income communities. A key target group for this policy would be non-married mothers and fathers around the time of the "magic moment" of a child's birth. This *CDA Report* demonstrates that policies to increase marriage among these parents could have a very large impact in reducing child poverty. In general, a 10 percent increase in marriage among poor single mothers would reduce child poverty within that group by 7 percentage points.

Healthy marriage is critical to the well-being of children, women, and men. President Bush's marriage-strengthening initiative should therefore be an essential part of any future welfare policy.

Promoting Marriage Would Not Reduce Poverty

by Paul Street

About the author: *Paul Street is a social policy researcher, freelance writer, and civil rights activist in Chicago, Illinois.*

Buried in the details of the regressive, militarist, and fiscally irresponsible budget plan released by the White House in early February [2002] is a weak but revealing proposal of marriage.[1] At this writing, the Bush administration is asking Congress for $100 million of federal welfare money to pay for experimental state programs to promote marriage among the nation's single welfare mothers. The proposal is based on the right-wing notion, trumpeted by reactionary think tanks like the Heritage Foundation, that the root causes of poverty and related alleged "welfare dependency" among the nation's most disadvantaged citizens are out-of-wedlock child births and the collapse of the traditional two-parent family. It's a convenient notion for policymakers who wish to avoid honest discussion of how the so-called welfare reform bill of 1996, which kicked millions of single mothers off public assistance and into the supposedly high-opportunity U.S. job market, has predictably worsened the plight of the nation's most disadvantaged children. That bill, titled the "Personal Responsibility and Work Opportunity Reconciliation Act" (PRA) was prefaced by the official Congressional "finding" that "marriage is the foundation of a successful society."

Superficial Statistics

Proponents of "marriage as the solution to poverty" wield a superficially impressive array of statistics showing that children born to unmarried parents are more likely to be born at a low birth weight, develop poor cognitive and verbal abilities, experience abuse, and "fail" in marriages than their counterparts in two parent homes. They cite solid and standard evidence that children in two-

---

1. As this volume went to press, this proposal had not passed.

parent families do better financially and emotionally than children in single-parent homes. They note that the majority of adult welfare recipients are single mothers struggling with the task of paying for children they lack the earnings to support. They conduct counterfactual "microsimulation analyses" to "show" that the child poverty rate would be 3 to 4 points lower if the "the proportion of children living in female-headed families [had] remained constant" rather than increasing from nearly 11 to more than 23 percent between 1970 and 1998.

Armed with such findings and with the often quite literally religious belief that the two-parent heterosexual family is the indispensable "foundation" of the good society, some state policymakers have already introduced a number of programs to promote marriage among the nation's disproportionately black and urban population of welfare moms. The measures include cash payments ($100 a month) to welfare mothers who tie the knot (West Virginia), marriage education for couples receiving welfare (Oklahoma), and marriage skills courses and a "healthy marriage handbook" for single welfare mothers (Arizona). [George W.] Bush hopes to make the expansion of such experiments across the country into a central component of the federal welfare bill. . . .

The influence of the idea that marriage is the solution to poverty in the Bush administration was evident [in the spring of 2001]. That's when the White House appointed Wade Horn, founder of the "pro-marriage" Fatherhood Initiative, to become Assistant Secretary for Family Support at the Department of Health and Human Services. Insisting that poor mothers are poor because they are not married, Horn has called for the federal government to give preference to children from two-parent families over children of single parents in admissions to the Head Start program.

Bush, Horn, and Heritage childishly confuse cause and effect when it comes to grasping fundamental relationships between poverty and family structure. It is one thing to find that children and families tend to do better, materially and otherwise, when they are organized along stable two-parent lines. Since correlation is not causation, however, it is quite another thing to extrapolate from that basic and uncontroversial finding to conclude that declining marriage and rising single motherhood are the causes of poverty and related alleged "welfare dependency."

The best poverty and family research suggests precisely the reverse, showing—and this finding was absent from the preface to the PRA—that the traditional family has been declining for the last 30 years under

> *"Welfare reform . . . has predictably worsened the plight of the nation's most disadvantaged children."*

the pressure of growing socioeconomic inequality. This polarization has made stable family life next to impossible for millions, especially those who lack the job skills and/or education and/or union protections required to make a livable wage. It has generated an all-too realistic sense of hopelessness on the part of disadvantaged rural and inner city youth, who see no future higher earnings or education to be endangered by engaging in pre-marital sex. It has been accompanied by rising rates of domestic violence and a relative decline of male earnings that has made men more dispensable in the minds of poor women seeking to escape abusive relationships—something with unintentionally positive consequences from a feminist perspective. It has also come alongside a related massive wave of arrest and incarceration directed especially at black males. The Bush marriage proposal says, in essence "let [the poor] eat wedding rings," to use the appropriately sarcastic phrase of Dorian Solot and Marshall Miller of the Alternatives to Marriage Project in Boston.

A Welfare Mother's Situation

Nothing reveals the sorry nature of Bush's marriage proposal more than the way these patterns have generated a critical shortage of both jobs and marriageable black males in those communities. To focus on the job issue, consider the situation of a hypothetical African-American welfare mother named Sharron Williams, 31 years old with 2 children and living in North Lawndale, a 99 percent African-American neighborhood on Chicago's West Side. Williams and her children could certainly use another adult breadwinner. Consistent with conservative claims, more than 27 percent of people in

> *"The traditional family has been declining for the last 30 years under the pressure of growing socioeconomic inequality."*

families headed by a single mother live beneath the federal government's poverty level, compared to 6.8 percent of people living in two-parent families. Even when single mothers work, the poverty rate for families headed by single mothers falls only to 19.4 percent.

Thanks to her location, education, gender, and race, it is likely that Sharron and her children are considerably poorer than the national population of single-mother households. Like more than 72 percent of the state's adult welfare recipients she lacks a high school degree. Like 73 percent of the same group she is African-American and like 98 percent she is female. It doesn't make for a terribly good labor market combination. According to the latest numbers from the U.S. Current Population Survey, black female high school dropouts have an average annual income, including public assistance, of $13,288. That is roughly consistent with the commonly reported median hourly earnings of former welfare recipients ($7.00 an hour). In Sharron's neighborhood, more than two-thirds of families are female-headed and just 13 percent of the residents have more than a high school education. Only 4 percent have more than 4 or more years of college and more than 4 in 10 people live below the poverty level.

We only begin to scratch the surface of Williams and her children's material difficulties by noting that her income is below the federal poverty level for a family of three ($14,600). Official U.S. poverty thresholds are absurdly low, based on a ridiculously antiquated formula that fails to make adequate space for the medical, childcare, transportation and other costs faced by people in the real world. That formula does not properly account for regional variations in the cost of living or for differential costs associated with variant family structures. A far better measure of Sharron's real cost of living is provided by the Economic Policy Institute's recent basic family budget estimate, calculated with the best available measures of minimally mainstream housing, food, clothing, childcare, transportation, tax and other costs and adjusted for geographical difference across every metropolitan area in the country. By EPI's calculation, it costs $35,307 dollars a year for a family of one parent and two children to meet basic family needs. Even if she lived in a less desperate neighborhood, Sharron's likely income would equal just more than a third of her family's real world requirements.

> *"It costs $35,307 dollars a year for a family of one parent and two children to meet basic family needs."*

A Shortage of Jobs

Sharron's chance of escaping poverty through employment is low. The job loss resulting from the current economic recession is both concentrated in the industries where many welfare recipients find employment and highly racialized. In December 2001 the official unemployment rate for black workers was 10.2 percent, up from 7.5 percent [in April 2001], nearly double that of whites, and it is considerably higher in the inner city. In Sharron's neighborhood at last full count, 27 percent of the civilian labor force was unemployed. Of the 22 Chicago neighborhoods that were more than 90 percent black in 1990, all had double-digit unemployment rates and 12 had rates of 20 percent and higher. Like the poverty rate, moreover, the official U.S. unemployment rate is deceptively optimistic. It deletes the considerable contingent of jobless people who have given up seeking work or never did so and leaves out part-time workers who would prefer to be full-time. It also omits the two million incarcerated Americans, half of whom are black.

Sharron's job possibilities did not improve much during the recently concluded "economic boom." Between 1991 and 2000, 98 percent of job growth in the Chicago metropolitan area took place in the predominantly white suburbs and not in the city, which houses two-thirds of the area's African-Americans. Slight employment expansion did occur in the city as a whole, but Chicago's 19 disproportionately black zip codes lost jobs during the "Clinton boom"[2] and the three zip codes covering North Lawndale lost nearly 3,000 jobs between 1991 and 2000.

---

2. a reference to the economic growth that occurred during Bill Clinton's presidency

At the end of the vaunted Clinton expansion, the Center for Labor Market Studies at Northeastern University reports, 30 percent of African-Americans ages 20 to 24 in the nation's 50 largest central cities were both out of school and out of work and 6 of every 10 African-Americans ages 16 to 24 in Chicago were jobless. Chicago, the Center found, was home to nearly 60,000 "disconnected" (out of school and work) 20–24 year olds, equivalent to nearly one in four of the city's young adults. The ratio was certainly much higher in the city's predominantly black and high poverty neighborhoods.

These findings are consistent with labor market research conducted by the Midwest Job Gap Project during the middle and late 1990s. In the Chicago metropolitan area, including even the relatively job-rich suburbs, the Project found, there was only one unskilled job opening in 1998 for every four unskilled workers who needed jobs, including former public assistance expected to find positions under the rules of welfare-to-work. In the city, there were more than 30 such workers for every unskilled job opening that paid at least poverty level wages for a family of three. This was in a period that saw the lowest official U.S. unemployment rate in more than 25 years.

Find a Man?

Likely to be frustrated in her struggle to achieve what policymakers like to call "self-sufficiency" through wage labor, Williams is free to follow the advice of the Heritage Foundation. Moving into what conservatives are now calling the "second phase" of welfare reform, from "get a job" to "get a husband," she can commence the search for a man.

One problem that quickly emerges and should concern even the most lukewarm feminist is that she probably has some very good experience-based reasons to be uninterested in that search. On the basis of a major research project that interviewed hundreds of inner city Chicago residents, Harvard sociologist William Julius Wilson reported, in *When Work Disappears* (1996), that "the relationships between inner city men and women, whether in a marital or nonmarital situation, are often fractious and antagonistic. Inner city black women routinely say that they distrust men and feel strongly that black men lack dedication to their families."

"The size of the pool of marriageable men in [poor black communities] is woefully inadequate."

Putting aside this by-no-means minor problem, the next roadblock on Williams's path to poverty-slashing marital bliss is the shortage of "marriageable" males in her immediate social milieu. Thanks to remarkably high and interrelated rates of unemployment, mortality, and incarceration in inner city neighborhoods, the size of the pool of marriageable men in Sharron's community is woefully inadequate. According to Wilson and other researchers, the increase in single mother black households since 1970 is directly related to a drastic decline in the "male marriageable pool index," defined as the ratio of employed men per 100 women of the same age and race, during the last third of the 20th century. Wilson discovered that that index fell from 67 to 44 for 24 year olds nationally between the early 1960s and 1980. At the heart of this decline, Wilson found, was the exodus of manufacturing employment from the central city, something that had a gravely disproportionate impact on the employment and earnings potential of black males.

At latest count from the Department of Labor, there are 63 employed black men 20 years and older for every 100 black females in the same age group. The comparable ratio of employed males to females in whites of the same age cohort is 84 to 100. For 20–24 year olds, the racial difference in employed males to same-race females is quite stark: 54 to 100 for blacks and 92 to 100 for whites. These are national level numbers however and the ratio is certainly far worse in neighborhoods like Sharron's. . . .

Where Welfare Moms Meet Ex-Cons

Many of Sharron's potential marriage partners are currently locked up in a sprawling prison-industrial complex that provides family-supporting jobs for predominantly white "down-state" communities far removed from the Chicago area. Between 1972 and 2000, the number of people behind bars in the United States rose from 330,000 to more than 2 million or 461 prisoners per 100,000 U.S. citizens. That rising and very disproportionately (nearly 50 percent) black, male (more than 90 percent), and urban-based population is now curiously roughly equivalent to the number of disproportionately black, female, and urban adult heads of welfare households. An estimated 11 percent of African-American males in their 20s and early 30s are incarcerated and on any given day 30 percent of African-American males ages 20 to 29 are "under correctional supervision": in prison or jail or on parole or probation. The Bureau of Justice Statistics has estimated that a young black man age 16 in 1996 faces a 29 percent chance of serving time in prison during his life. In predominantly black inner-city communities across the nation, incarceration has become so commonplace that it has become something of a "normative experience" ("no big deal") for black males. Seven percent of the nation's black children have at least one parent behind bars.

> *"[Ex-felons] emerge . . . unprepared to engage as loving husbands or fathers."*

A recent *Time* magazine article reports that more than 630,000 people, half of them black, will be released from prison in 2002—the largest prison exodus in history. A hugely disproportionate number of these ex-offenders will be returning to a relatively small number of high-poverty inner-city neighborhoods, which also provide leading concentrations of single mother welfare households. Numerous studies have pegged these ex-offenders' "unemployable" rate at higher than 60 percent. The minority of those who find "legitimate" work, *Time* reports, have done so in low paying "off-the-books" jobs.

Sharron's city, neighborhood, and state are no exceptions to the national pattern. In Illinois, home to the third largest population of prisoners in the nation, the prison population has grown by more than 60 percent since 1990. More than 60 percent of the state's nearly 46,000 prisoners are black males. Seventy percent of these black male prisoners come from the Chicago metropolitan area, where Chicago's Cook County is home to 81 percent of the state's adult female welfare recipients, up from 64 percent in 1995, when welfare "reform" was moving into high gear at the state level. According to a recent analysis by the *Chicago Reporter*, 1 in 5 black men ages 20 to 29 in Cook County are either in prison or jail or on parole. For Cook County whites of the same gender and age, the corresponding ratio is 1 in 104. As of . . . June [2001], there were nearly 20,000 more black males in the Illinois state prison system than the number of black males enrolled in the state's public universities. There are more black males in the state prisons than in all of the state's post-secondary educational institutions including community colleges. Seventy percent of the men between ages 18 and 45 in Sharron's neighborhood are ex-offenders.

> *"It does not follow that marriage would end poverty among unmarried couples."*

Nearly 50 percent of the state's African-Americans released from prison return within at least 3 years. They carry what many of them call an "X" on their backs—a felony conviction that is readily evident to the 49 percent of American employers that conduct criminal background checks on potential employees and of whom more than half report that they never hire ex-offenders. They emerge equally unprepared to engage as loving husbands or fathers.

It's all part of a self-defeating "feedback" loop that has been deepening over time. Directly related to the economic marginalization of black males in postindustrial America, the decline of the two-parent inner-city family is strongly associated with urban violence (itself a major contributor to black male mortality) and crime. As "family disruption" increases, sociologist Robert Sampson notes, the "community social ties" and "informal networks of social control" that tend to keep younger black males out of illegal activities collapse. This feeds high urban crime rates that are exaggerated to provide the pretext for the rise of a racially disparate mass-incarceration state that decreases yet more the ratio of urban black males to females and deepens the economic and social-psychological incapacitation of black males.

What If Poor Parents Got Married?

[In 2001], Princeton University researchers using data from the Fragile Families Wellbeing Study examined nearly 5,000 births to unmarried mothers in 20 large U.S. cities, analyzing age, educational, wage and other factors to estimate likely outcomes if the mothers got married to the fathers of their children. In counterfactual scenarios where the female of the newly married pair stayed home, they found that 22 percent of the families would be below the poverty line and 59 percent would be below 150 percent of the poverty level. Even if both of the newly married parents were to work outside home, they determined, 28 percent of the families would still be below poverty. Part of the explanation for these poor outcomes, the Princeton team found, was that unmarried parents are considerably younger and have less education and earnings potential than married parents.

"Yes," concludes Solot and Miller, "on average married couples are less likely to be poor than unmarried couples. But it does not follow that marriage would end poverty among unmarried couples." The latter's often considerable economic difficulties "cannot," according to the Princeton researchers, "be magically altered by a marriage license." Consistent with this conclusion, there is little correlation between marriage and child poverty rates on an international scale. Solot and Miller note that "the four countries with some of the lowest child poverty rates in Europe (Sweden, Norway, Denmark, and France) all have unmarried birth rates far higher than the United States. Sweden's child poverty rate is seven times lower than the rate in the U.S., despite the fact that the majority of babies there are born to unmarried parents." The main difference is the presence of social-democratic welfare states in the European nations and the related prevalence in those nations of the judgment that children born into a family and world they never made should not grow up in poverty. Blaming single-parenthood for poverty is an elite American mechanism for avoiding the inhumane consequences of the disturbing fact that U.S. policy makers do not share that judgment. . . .

Curious Facts

Ignored by the Bush team is the fact the combined percentage of poor and near-poor (twice the poverty level) children living in single-mother households actually fell between 1995 and 2000. The reduction likely reflected the moderate increase in family-enabling wages for lesser skilled workers that occurred during the second half of the Clinton boom. It suggests that the single-motherhood "problem" was declining when Bush and his conservative anti-social policy advisers

> *"There is little correlation between marriage and child poverty rates on an international scale."*

seized the White House with a little family assistance from five partisan Supreme Court justices.

It is curious also to note that welfare reform has long been justified by the widely propagated and dear-to-Republicans' belief that the expansion of liberal welfare policies and rising benefit levels during and after the 1960s provided the chief cause of the rise of female-headed families and the out-of-wedlock births. Interesting, then, that five years after the abolition of the welfare entitle-ment, with public family assistance caseloads at less than half their mid-1990s level, the "problem" of the poor female-headed family remains very much alive and well in the minds of policymakers. Perhaps this is part of why the Bush ad-ministration is not putting all that much money into its marriage proposal to welfare mothers. The White House is not exactly going all out for the engage-ment ring. It wants to pay for the marriage experiments by eliminating the inef-fective financial bonuses (paid out of welfare dollars) the federal government has been giving to states that reduce out-of-wedlock births across the board.

Smart and Mean

Still, Bush's proposal is reflective of the real White House agenda. More mean than stupid, that agenda has nothing to do with solving poverty or easing the crisis of poor families. It is shaped by some very different and interrelated priorities greatly assisted by the [terrorist attacks of September 11, 2001] and the fear and repression they engendered. More than slightly reminiscent of the [Ronald] Reagan years, those priorities are to distribute wealth yet further up-ward, to reward big money corporate campaign contributors, to expand the mil-itary budget like never before, to eviscerate social expenditures, and to keep the religious right on board.

From the perspective of these goals, the marriage proposal is smart and incredibly cheap. It shifts responsi-bility for taking care of poor children from government and the capitalist

> *"[Promoting marriage to reduce poverty] shifts responsibility for taking care of poor children . . . to society's truest victims."*

labor market to society's truest victims and does so in a time when poverty is dramatically on the rise. It is advertised in a way that addresses the qualms of politically significant social moderates by creating an illusion of compassionate concern for the plight of the poor. It throws a bone to the ever-valuable political dogs of the sexist "family values" right, for whom the single-mother-headed household is an abomination in and of itself, whatever its real relationship to poverty. It diverts attention from the real causes of poverty, focusing voters and obedient media lapdogs on the "irresponsible" behavior of the poor. Better to focus on the victims than the forces of economic irequity and race and gender discrimination and the irresponsible behaviors and values of "elite" citizens that combine to generate misery at the bottom of a savagely unequal social struc-ture. Countering those forces would require a level of public and social invest-ment that is anathema to conventional neo-liberal policy wisdom and particu-larly ruled out by Bush's commitment to slashing taxes for and funneling billions of dollars to his super-opulent friends and corporate paymasters. Seen in the context of the overall agenda of which it is part, Bush's sorry little mar-riage proposal is very smart indeed.

The Affluent Should Give a Large Portion of Their Income to the Poor

by Peter Singer

About the author: *Peter Singer is a philosopher and ethicist who teaches at Princeton University.*

In the Brazilian film *Central Station*, Dora is a retired schoolteacher who makes ends meet by sitting at the station writing letters for illiterate people. Suddenly she has an opportunity to pocket $1,000. All she has to do is persuade a 9-year-old homeless boy to follow her to an address she has been given. (She is told he will be adopted by wealthy foreigners.) She delivers the boy, gets the money, spends some of it on a television set, and settles down to enjoy her new acquisition. Her neighbor spoils the fun, however, by telling her that the boy was too old to be adopted—he will be killed and his organs sold for transplantation. Perhaps Dora knew this all along, but after her neighbor's plain speaking, she spends a troubled night. In the morning Dora resolves to take the boy back.

Suppose Dora had told her neighbor that it is a tough world, other people have nice new TVs too, and if selling the kid is the only way she can get one, well, he was only a street kid. She would then have become, in the eyes of the audience, a monster. She redeems herself only by being prepared to bear considerable risks to save the boy.

At the end of the movie, in cinemas in the affluent nations of the world, people who would have been quick to condemn Dora if she had not rescued the boy go home to places far more comfortable than her apartment. In fact, the average family in the United States spends almost one-third of its income on things that are no more necessary to them than Dora's new TV was to her. Going out to nice restaurants, buying new clothes because the old ones are no longer stylish, vacationing at beach resorts—so much of our income is spent on things not essential to the preservation of our lives and health. Donated to a

Peter Singer, "Why You Should Give Away Most of Your Money," *Medical Economics*, vol. 76, November 8, 1999, p. 275. Copyright © 1999 by Peter Singer. Reproduced by permission.

number of charitable agencies, that money could mean the difference between life and death for children in need.

A Serious Moral Issue

All of which raises a question: In the end, what's the ethical distinction between a Brazilian who sells a homeless child to organ peddlers and an American who already has a TV and upgrades to a better one—knowing that the money could be donated to an organization that would use it to save the lives of children in need?

Of course, there are several differences between the two situations that could support different moral judgments about them. For one thing, to be able to consign a child to death when he is standing right in front of you takes a chilling kind of heartlessness: it is much easier to ignore an appeal for money to help children you will never meet. Yet for a utilitarian philosopher like myself—that is, one who judges whether acts are right or wrong by their consequences—if the upshot of the American's failure to donate the money is that one more kid dies on the streets of a Brazilian city, then it is, in some sense, just as bad as selling the kid to the organ peddlers. But one doesn't need to embrace my utilitarian ethic to see that, at the very least, there is a troubling incongruity in being so quick to condemn Dora for taking the child to the organ peddlers while, at the same time, not regarding the American consumer's behavior as raising a serious moral issue.

In his 1996 book, *Living High and Letting Die*, the New York University philosopher Peter Unger presented an ingenious series of imaginary examples designed to probe our intuitions about whether it is wrong to live well without giving substantial amounts of money to help people who are hungry, malnourished, or dying from easily treatable illnesses, like diarrhea. Here's my paraphrase of one of these examples:

Bob is close to retirement. He has invested most of his savings in a very rare and valuable old car, a Bugatti, which he has not been able to insure. The Bugatti is his pride and joy. In addition to the pleasure he gets from driving and caring for his car, Bob knows that its rising market value means that he will always be able to sell it and live comfortably after retirement. One day when Bob is out for a drive, he parks the Bugatti near the end of a railway siding and goes for a walk up the track. As he does so, he sees that a

> *"So much of our income is spent on things not essential to . . . our lives and health."*

runaway train, with no one aboard, is running down the railway track. Looking farther down the track, he sees the small figure of a child very likely to be killed by the runaway train. He can't stop the train and the child is too far away to warn of the danger, but he can throw a switch that will divert the train down the siding where his Bugatti is parked. Then nobody will be killed—but the train will destroy his Bugatti. Thinking of his joy in owning the car and the financial security it represents, Bob decides not to throw the switch. The child is killed. For many years to come, Bob enjoys owning his Bugatti and the financial security it represents.

Bob's conduct, most of us will immediately respond, was gravely wrong. Unger agrees. But then he reminds us that we, too, have opportunities to save the lives of children. We can give to organizations like Unicef and Oxfam America. How much would we have to give to one of these organizations to have a high probability of saving the life of a child threatened by an easily preventable disease? (I do not believe that children are more worth saving than adults, but since no one can argue that children have brought their poverty on themselves, focusing on them simplifies the issues.) Unger called up some experts and used the information they provided to offer some plausible estimates that included the cost of raising money, administrative expenses, and the cost of delivering aid where it is most needed. By his calculation, $200 in donations would help a sickly 2-year-old transform into a healthy 6-year old—offering safe passage through childhood's most dangerous years. To show how practical philosophical argument can be, Unger even tells his readers that they can easily donate funds by calling one of these toll-free numbers: 800-367-5437 for Unicef: 800-693-2687 for Oxfam America.

> *"The American consumer's behavior [raises] a serious moral issue."*

Now you, too, have the information you need to save a child's life. How should you judge yourself if you don't do it? Think again about Bob and his Bugatti. Unlike Dora, Bob did not have to look into the eyes of the child he was sacrificing for his own material comfort. The child was a complete stranger to him and too far away to relate to in an intimate, personal way. Unlike Dora, too, he did not mislead the child or initiate the chain of events imperiling him. In all these respects, Bob's situation resembles that of people able but unwilling to donate to overseas aid and differs from Dora's situation.

Ethical Distinctions?

If you still think that it was very wrong of Bob not to throw the switch that would have diverted the train and saved the child's life, then it is hard to see how you could deny that it is also very wrong not to send money to one of the organizations listed above. Unless, that is, there is some morally important difference between the two situations that I have overlooked.

Is it the practical uncertainties about whether aid will really reach the people who need it? Nobody who knows the world of overseas aid can doubt that such uncertainties exist. But Unger's figure of $200 needed to save a child's life was reached after he had made conservative assumptions about the proportion of the money donated that will actually reach its target.

One genuine difference between Bob and those who can afford to donate to overseas aid organizations but don't is that only Bob can save the child on the tracks, whereas there are hundreds of millions of people who can give $200 to overseas aid organizations. The problem is that most of them aren't doing it. Does this mean that it is all right for you not to do it?

Suppose that there were more owners of priceless vintage cars—Carol, Dave, Emma, Fred, and so on, down

> *"Each one of us with wealth surplus . . . should be giving most of it to help people suffering from poverty."*

to Ziggy—all in exactly the same situation as Bob, with their own siding and their own switch, all sacrificing the child in order to preserve their own precious car. Would that make it all right for Bob to do the same? To answer this question affirmatively is to endorse follow-the-crowd ethics—the kind of ethics that led many Germans to look away when Nazi atrocities were being committed. We do not excuse them because others were behaving no better.

We seem to lack a sound basis for drawing a clear moral line between Bob's situation and that of any reader of this article with $200 to spare who does not donate it to an overseas aid agency. These readers seem to be acting at least as badly as Bob was acting when he chose to let the runaway train hurtle toward the unsuspecting child. In the light of this conclusion. I trust that many readers will reach for the phone and donate the $200. Perhaps you should do it before reading further.

When Should Giving Stop?

Now that you have distinguished yourself morally from people who put their vintage cars ahead of a child's life, how about treating yourself and your partner to dinner at a favorite restaurant? But wait. The money you will spend at the restaurant could also help save the lives of children overseas! True, you weren't planning to blow $200 tonight, but if you were to give up dining out for just one month, you would easily save that amount. And what is one month's dining out, compared to a child's life? There's the rub. Since there are a lot of desperately needy children in the world, there will always be another child whose life you could save for another $200. Are you therefore obliged to keep giving until you have nothing left? At what point can you stop?

Hypothetical examples can easily become farcical. Consider Bob. How far past losing the Bugatti should he go? Imagine that Bob had got his foot stuck in the track of the siding, and if he diverted the train, then before it rammed the car it would also amputate his big toe. Should he still throw the switch? What if it would amputate his foot? His entire leg?

As absurd as the Bugatti scenario gets when pushed to extremes, the point it raises is a serious one: Only when the sacrifices become very significant indeed would most people be prepared to say that Bob does nothing wrong when he decides not to throw the switch. Of course, most people could be wrong; we can't decide moral issues by taking opinion polls. But consider for yourself the level of sacrifice that you would demand of Bob, and then think about how much money you would have to give away in order to make a sacrifice that is roughly equal to that. It's almost certainly much, much more than $200. For most middle-class Americans, it could easily be more like $200,000.

Isn't it counterproductive to ask people to do so much? Don't we run the risk that many will shrug their shoulders and say that morality, so conceived, is fine for saints but not for them? I accept that we are unlikely to see, in the near or even medium-term fixture, a world in which it is normal for wealthy Americans to give the bulk of their wealth to strangers. When it comes to praising or blaming people for what they do, we tend to use a standard that is relative to some conception of normal behavior. Comfortably off Americans who give, say, 10 percent of their income to overseas aid organizations are so far ahead of most of their equally comfortable fellow citizens that I wouldn't go out of my way to chastise them for not doing more. Nevertheless, they should be doing much more, and they are in no position to criticize Bob for failing to make the much greater sacrifice of his Bugatti.

Various Objections

At this point various objections may crop up. Someone may say: If every citizen living in the affluent nations contributed his or her share I wouldn't have to make such a drastic sacrifice, because long before such levels were reached, the resources would have been there to save the lives of all those children dying from lack of food or medical care. So why should I give more than my fair share? Another, related objection is that the government ought to increase its overseas aid allocations, since that would spread the burden more equitably across all taxpayers.

Yet the question of how much we should give is a matter to be decided in the real world—and that, sadly, is a world in which we know that most people do not, and in the immediate future will not, give substantial amounts to overseas aid agencies. We know, too, that at least in the next year, the United States government is not going to meet even the very modest United Nations–recommended target of 0.7 percent of gross national product; at the moment, it lags far below that, at 0.09 percent, not even half of Japan's 0.22 percent or a tenth of Denmark's 0.97 percent. Thus, we know that the money we can give beyond that theoretical "fair share" is still going to save lives that would otherwise be lost. While the idea that no one need do more than his or her fair share is a powerful one, should it prevail if we know that others are not doing their fair share and that children will die preventable deaths unless we do more than our fair share? That would be taking fairness too far.

> *"A $1,000 suit could save five children's lives."*

Thus, this ground for limiting how much we ought to give also fails. In the world as it is now, I can see no escape from the conclusion that each one of us with wealth surplus to his or her essential needs should be giving most of it to help people suffering from poverty so dire as to be life-threatening. That's right: I'm saying that you shouldn't buy that new car, take that cruise, redecorate the house, or get that pricey new suit. After all, a $1,000 suit could save five children's lives.

So how does my philosophy break down in dollars and cents? An American household with an income of $50,000 spends around $30,000 annually on necessities, according to the Conference Board, a nonprofit economic research organization. Therefore, for a household bringing in $50,000 a year, donations to help the world's poor should come as close as possible to $20,000. The $30,000 required for necessities holds for higher incomes as well. So a household making $100,000 could cut a yearly check for $70,000. Again, the formula is simple: Whatever money you're spending on luxuries, not necessities, should be given away.

Now, evolutionary psychologists tell us that human nature just isn't sufficiently altruistic to make it plausible that many people will sacrifice so much for strangers. On the facts of human nature, they might be right, but they would be wrong to draw a moral conclusion from those facts. If it is the case that we ought to do things that, predictably, most of us won't do, then let's face that fact head-on. Then, if we value the life of a child more than going to fancy restaurants, the next time we dine out we will know that we could have done something better with our money. If that makes living a morally decent life extremely arduous, well, then that is the way things are. If we don't do it, then we should at least know that we are failing to live a morally decent life—not because it is good to wallow in guilt but because knowing where we should be going is the first step toward heading in that direction.

> *"Whatever money you're spending on luxuries, not necessities, should be given away."*

When Bob first grasped the dilemma that faced him as he stood by that railway switch, he must have thought how extraordinarily unlucky he was to be placed in a situation in which he must choose between the life of an innocent child and the sacrifice of most of his savings. But he was not unlucky at all. We are all in that situation.

The Affluent Should Not Give Money to the Poor

by Walter Williams

About the author: *Walter Williams is a nationally syndicated columnist.*

How many times have we heard people being applauded for "giving back"?

People seem to believe that, if you've been successful and made a lot of money, you're somehow obliged to give back by making donations to this or that cause, program or people. Giving back is not only a nonsensical idea but a dangerous one, as well. It reflects ignorance about the sources of income and at the same time provides fuel for demagogues and charlatans.

The Sources of Income

Depending on one's vision of the sources of income, giving back not only makes good sense but is a moral imperative, as well. Suppose income was simply a huge pile of money that was meant to be distributed equally. The reason some people are rich and others are not is because greedy rich people got to the pile first and took an unfair share. Giving back would be the right thing to do.

Another vision of the sources of income might be that income is distributed. In other words, there is a dealer of dollars. In this case, the reason why some people are rich and others are not is that the dollar dealer is a racist, a sexist or a multinationalist. Those to whom the mean dealer dealt too large a share of dollars should give back some of their ill-gotten gains. If they refuse to give back, then it's the job of government to confiscate their gains and return them to their rightful owners. In a word, there must be a redealing of the dollars, what some call income redistribution.

In a free society, income is neither taken nor distributed, it is earned. Income is earned by pleasing one's fellow man. The greater one's ability to please his fellow man, the greater is his claim on what his fellow man produces. This claim is represented by the size of his income.

Let's look at it. Say I mow your lawn. When I'm finished, you pay me $20. I

Walter Williams, "Giving Back Is Illogical," *Conservative Chronicle*, vol. 17, March 20, 2003, p. 21.
Copyright © 2003 by *Conservative Chronicle*. Reproduced by permission of Creators Syndicate.

go to my grocer and demand, "Give me two pounds of sirloin and a six-pack of beer that my fellow man produced." The grocer asks, "Williams, what did you do to deserve a claim on what your fellow man produced?" I say, "I served him." The grocer says, "Prove it." That's when I pull out the $20 I earned. We might think of those 20 dollars as "certificates of performance," evidence of service.

Free markets—along with peaceable, voluntary exchange—are morally superior to other alternatives. In order to make a claim on what my fellow man produces, I must serve him. Contrast that principle to government handouts, where a person is told: "You don't have to serve your fellow man. We'll take what he produces and give it to you."

> *"In a free society, income is neither taken nor distributed, it is earned."*

Michael Jackson is rich. So is Steve Jobs and Michael Jordan. Henry Ford was rich, and so was Jonas Salk—but not Williams. Why? I can sing. I can also play basketball. The problem is that my fellow man is not as pleased by my performance as he is with Michael Jackson and Michael Jordan. Henry Ford became rich by making it possible for the ordinary person to own a car, and Jonas Salk helped eliminate a dreaded disease. You tell me what else do they owe anyone? They've already given.

Who Should Give Back?

In our society, there are people who should give back. These are the thieves and social parasites who live forcibly at the expense of others. They prey on their fellow man. Some do it privately through theft, fraud and robbery. Others use the political mechanism whereby Congress enriches them at the expense of others. If giving back means anything, it should apply to thieves and social parasites, not those who became wealthy by serving us.

Increased Access to Shelters Would Help the Homeless

by Ralph da Costa Nunez and Laura M. Caruso

About the author: *Ralph da Costa Nunez is president and CEO of Homes for the Homeless in New York. Laura M. Caruso is the director of management and budget for Homes for the Homeless.*

Family homelessness is undergoing a marked transformation and entering a new stage of unprecedented growth. After shifting from an emergency housing problem in the early 1980s to one of sustained poverty during the 1990s, homelessness is on the verge of taking yet another turn. Limitations on the availability of public assistance and a booming, then faltering, economy have destabilized millions of families and ultimately forced thousands into homelessness.

Twenty years ago, one-time housing emergencies—fires, hazardous living conditions, and personal calamities—were the primary cause of family homelessness. Forced out of their homes, families required short-term emergency shelter until they were able to locate new housing. Because of the Reagan Administration's reductions in housing subsidies and social service programs, followed by the welfare reforms of the 1990s, homelessness grew tremendously, taking on an entirely new dimension. On average, homeless families are substantially younger, less educated, and poorer than those of the 1980s. In essence, an entire generation has been notched down into a chronic poverty that claims homelessness as one of its most defining characteristics.

The Causes of Homelessness

For many, homelessness is not simply a housing issue. Rather, it stems from poor education, lack of employable skills, inadequate health care, domestic violence, child abuse, foster care, and insufficient child care. Many of today's homeless families are headed by a young unmarried mother, with two or three children. She grew up in poverty, may have experienced domestic violence, and never completed high school, often dropping out due to pregnancy. She has at least one child suffering from a chronic health problem and has had trouble enrolling her kids in school. She has lived with a relative or partner, or doubled-up prior to becoming homeless, and left her last residence due to overcrowding, a disagreement, or violence. She currently is unemployed

> *"Over the last three decades, the stock of affordable housing has declined significantly."*

due to a lack of work skills or child care—or both—and is dependent on public assistance to support herself and her family.

As for the children, homelessness is usually not a brief or singular experience—27% have been homeless more than once, living in at least three different residences in a single year. Without permanent housing, such youngsters endure frequent moves—at a rate 16 times that of the typical American family—from motels to doubled-up apartments with family or friends to shelters. On average, they are homeless 10 months at a time, or an entire school year, a period fraught with educational and emotional setbacks. Nationally, 20% repeat a grade in school and 16% are enrolled in special education classes—rates 100% and 33%, respectively, higher than their nonhomeless peers. More than half change schools once a year, and over one-third switch two or more times, setting them back at least six months each time.

Today in America, over 600,000 families and more than 1,000,000 children are homeless, living in shelters, on the streets, in cars, and on campgrounds. According to the U.S. Conference of Mayors, requests for emergency shelter by families increased an average of 22% in 2001 and 17% the year before. After 20 years of steady increases and with additional changes in welfare reform again on the table, why shouldn't we expect more of the same? Isn't it time to move in a new direction? First, though, it is necessary to understand the primary factors that have contributed to this dramatic rise—a shortage of affordable housing, a decrease in jobs paying a living wage, and welfare reform. What these trends reveal is a new era of homelessness dominated by a growing class of Americans living for long periods in shelters.

The Housing Crisis

Over the last three decades, the stock of affordable housing has declined significantly, so that, by 1995, the gap between low-income renters and low-cost rental units, nonexistent in 1970, widened to more than 4,400,000. From 1996 to 1998, the most-recent data available, the situation worsened as the number of affordable units further decreased by 19%, or 1,300,000 units, due to the demolition of distressed properties and a shift of privately owned subsidized units to open-rental market rates.

In response to these trends, more families are forced to pay a larger share of their income in rent. In the last 20 years, the proportion of households with children paying more than 30% of their income on housing rose from 15 to 28%—a burden that the Federal government reports places low-income families at risk of homelessness. Today, 6,000,000 households, with over 4,000,000 children, have worst-case housing needs, earning less than 50% of the local median income and either paying more than half of their income in rent, living in severely substandard housing, or both. As a result, millions of children and their families are living on the brink of homelessness with no alternative.

Also contributing to the housing crisis and to homelessness is the decreasing value of wages. From 1979 to 1999, the most-recent data available, hourly salary for low-wage workers fell nine percent, adjusted for inflation—the result of a shift away from higher-paying manufacturing jobs to lower-paying service positions. These are typically very-low-wage or part-time jobs with few or no benefits, leaving employees with minimal resources to care for their families. For example, in 2000, a full-time worker earning minimum wage could not afford the fair-market rent for a two-bedroom apartment anywhere in the U.S. Instead, his or her family is first forced into a doubled-up living situation, then ultimately to a shelter.

The Effects of Welfare Reform

This economic shift is particularly sobering in light of recent . . . welfare policy changes. More than 9,000,000 people (two-thirds of them children) have left the welfare rolls since 1994—a 68% reduction in caseloads. As families leave public assistance, they are forced into a competitive low-wage market. A Center on Budget and Policy Priorities report found that those who find jobs after welfare typically earn between $8,000 and $10,800 annually—well below the poverty line of $14,129 for a family of three. Considering the average fair-market rents, those leaving public assistance could end up paying between 50 and 75% of their income on housing.

Moreover, welfare reductions have directly fueled homelessness. In a study of 22 cities, 37% of families had their welfare benefits reduced or cut in the last year, with 20% becoming homeless as a result. Most strikingly, in Philadelphia and Seattle, more than 50% had their benefits reduced or cut and, among those, 42 and 38%, respectively, became homeless as a result. A second study of six states found that, within six months of families losing their welfare benefits, 25% doubled-up on housing to save money and 23% moved because they could not afford

> *"Millions of children and their families are living on the brink of homelessness with no alternative."*

rent. In San Diego County, welfare reform not only resulted in homelessness, but in disintegrated families, as 18% of those parents whose benefits were reduced or cut lost a child to foster care. With the full impact of time limits yet to come, the ongoing effects of welfare reform highlight the changing state of homelessness.

More and more families are seeking subsidized housing at a time following 20 years of reduced Federal support. In 1986, for the first time ever, Federal outlays for housing assistance fell more than 50%, from $80,000,000 to $38,000,000, never again achieving an adequate level of support. In 1995, the number of Federally assisted households fell and no new units of assistance were funded for four years. As a result, lengthy waiting lists for Section 8 housing, a Federal program that gives incentives to landlords to provide low-income housing and rent subsidies as well as for public housing are now the norm. Between 1998 and 1999 alone, the most-recent data available, Section 8 waiting lists increased by 34%. In Los Angeles and Newark, N.J., the wait for Section 8 is 10 years, and 52% of all homeless families in America are on subsidized housing waiting lists.

> *"Those leaving public assistance could end up paying between 50 and 75% of their income on housing."*

Clearly, the stage has been set for yet another generation of homeless families. While we continue to demand the development of new affordable housing, it is not on the horizon, and for many families, housing alone is not sufficient. Those who have worked closely with homeless families know that many need supportive services in order to maintain their own home, hold a job, and live independently. So, why not offer supportive housing with services? Government is not building significant levels of low-income housing and, whether intentional or not, has spent billions of dollars over many years erecting a massive shelter system across America. These shelters have become homes to over 1,000,000 kids and their families. Without alternatives, the homeless find themselves turning to shelters as the one remaining element of a dwindling safety net, often as a last resort to keep their families together. Yet, it is here—in shelters—that the reduction of family homelessness may actually begin.

A Catalyst for Reducing Homelessness

Shelters and transitional housing themselves may be the catalyst for reducing homelessness by providing on-site services and programs that address the root causes of this new poverty. By using the national shelter infrastructure already in place to provide immediate housing—given the history of paltry housing options in the face of an economic boom and especially in light of a new national focus on homeland security—we can enhance services to be comprehensive and focused on building long-term skills that foster independence and economic viability. If we take the emergency out of the situation and allow them to focus on building real skills and work histories, we offer families their first step on a path to self-determination.

Fifteen years ago, shelters were stark, temporary, scary places, as families lived in congregate settings, on cots huddled together in an open space. They were gymnasiums, armories, and church basements—none an appropriate place to call home. However, many of today's shelters are different. They have private rooms with cooking facilities; some are apartments with one or two bedrooms, which are safe, clean, and offer a multitude of services. In fact, these shelters are becoming surrogate communities, places from which parents commute to work and children go to school. (Twenty-six percent of families in shelters are currently employed.) Many provide child care and after-school programs for youngsters, and job-readiness training and life skills for adults. They are places where parents are raising their families and that have become home to those who live there.

In a shelter-turned-community, directors should advocate for resources for their residents just like elected officials do for their constituents, and staff must link families to a variety of educational and employment options just like guidance counselors do for their students. For homeless families, a stay in the shelter community could be a second chance to advance literacy levels, finish high school, build a work history, and enhance life skills, and this is only the beginning. They can be expanded and financed through housing assistance vouchers targeted to them; residents who work could pay some rent; and partnerships with the public and private sectors could further enrich services. The more comprehensive the network of shelter-based services, the more vibrant and effective this community becomes.

The acceptance and expansion of such a plan—putting shelter communities to work to reduce family homelessness—requires bold leadership and vision. Yet, it can be done, and, in many instances, the process has already begun. A real and meaningful plan to end family homelessness in this country must begin by being politically honest with the American people. Government has not and, in all likelihood, will not be producing low-income homing on any acceptable level in the near future. Instead, we are going to have to acknowledge that, for the time being, a shelter is indeed a home, and one that must continue to evolve into a community with opportunities.

Handouts Often Harm the Homeless

by Amy L. Sherman

About the author: *Amy L. Sherman is director of urban ministries at Trinity Presbyterian Church in Charlottesville, Virginia.*

A few months ago, I knowingly harmed an indigent woman named Jacqueline. She was standing at the end of the exit ramp, holding up the predictable sign: "Homeless. Please Help." I parked the car and doubled back to talk to her. She and her "old man" had come from a city a few hours east, she said. For the last few day's they'd been sleeping under a small cluster of leafy trees a stone's throw from the Interstate.

I tried hard to persuade Jacqueline to let me take her to the Salvation Army shelter. I knew its directors and something of its programs and could attest to its safety and cleanliness. Jacqueline was adamantly opposed. In a few minutes I recognized that she wasn't quite all there mentally. Further debate was fruitless. And so I did what I almost never do. I gave Jacqueline a handout.

We got into my car and I drove her to Food Lion. I told her to pick out what she needed and I'd buy. Her desires were modest: a pack of hot dogs, a bottle of Pepsi, canned meat, a loaf of white bread and a tiny bottle of Texas Pete hot sauce. I urged fruit and vegetables on her to no avail. Then we stopped at the Family Dollar store, where she selected a cheap bra and two pairs of underpants. Bug spray from CVS completed our shopping expedition, and I drove her back to her "campsite."

I visited her and her husband there a couple more times over ensuing days, offering him tips on grounds-keeping jobs and continually suggesting they visit the Salvation Army shelter. I guess they've moved on, since I haven't seen them for over a month.

I'm convinced that handouts are basically wrongheaded. A recent book by James L. Payne, *Overcoming Welfare*, makes the case against them particularly well. Handouts, he says, demean recipients by implying that beneficiaries can't

Amy L. Sherman, "Expectant Giving," *Christian Century*, vol. 116, February 24, 1999, p. 206.

meet their own needs. They can enable dysfunctional behavior and can be disincentives to work. By contrast, "expectant giving"—a contribution that demands a constructive response from the supplicant—affirms people's God-given dignity and capacities. It's a "hand-up," not a handout.

Most Americans favor hand-ups. We don't wish to reward people for irresponsibility or engender dependency among the able-bodied. Ironically, though, most of our social welfare systems (public and private) offer handouts, not hand-ups. Payne offers several explanations for this.

First, hand-up giving requires far more time, thought and personal investment than sympathetic (handout) giving. It's much easier to toss the homeless a few dollars than to build a relationship with them [that] can address the root causes of their condition. Second, donors (especially religiously motivated ones) sometimes misapply maxims about giving, like the story of the Good Samaritan. As Payne explains, "Our homilies and parables are right to encourage our generosity towards strangers in unexpected situations. But these teachings don't tell us how to act if we are asked to give a second time." Yet we often use the Good Samaritan example to justify programs of repeated giving (like Food Stamps). Third, governments tend inevitably to provide sympathetic, rather than expectant, giving. Government bureaucracies are distant from individual poor families and cannot properly assess their particular needs or respond flexibly—two requirements of expectant giving. Moreover, bureaucracies are loath to make the kind of judgments expectant giving demands. They tend to operate explicitly on the principle that no lifestyle is superior to another.

> *"I'm convinced that handouts are basically wrongheaded."*

For all these reasons, Payne laments, we keep giving indiscriminately and thoughtlessly, to the detriment of the poor. And our affluence provides us the means to keep on killing with kindness. Payne's words are cutting, but generally true: "The routinized giving of material assistance to strangers must be seen as a vice, not as a praiseworthy activity."

Expectant Giving

The quid pro quo of expectant giving sounds off-putting to religiously attuned ears. But hard-working, devout charity workers in the 19th century practiced it regularly. Consider Octavia Hill, who lived among the poor in the low-income apartment complexes she managed in London. Hill refused any salary for this work and poured her heart and soul into the children and adults she mentored for four decades. Her essays on her experiences are saturated with the delight she felt in this work, the love she gave and received, and the obvious respect she had for others' dignity. Her writings also make crystal clear her devotion to tough love and accountability and her unwillingness to engage in indiscriminate charity that engendered dependency. She challenged donors to consider whether their giving was not only benevolent in its intent but also beneficient in its long-term result. How well do our church-based soup kitchens live up to this?

I consider Octavia Hill a mentor and insist that the ministry I direct in a low-income urban neighborhood operate on the principles of expectant giving. Nevertheless, I gave Jacqueline a handout. Why?

Shortly before meeting Jacqueline I had conducted a lengthy interview with Felicia, a woman in our job training program. I learned that my church had been involved with Felicia for several years prior to her enrollment in our program. The church had paid her bills on occasion and linked her with a mentor. After several months, Felicia abandoned that relationship and tried again to make her own way. That flopped, and Felicia found herself facing a turn-off notice from the electric company because of unpaid bills.

> *"We keep giving indiscriminately and thoughtlessly, to the detriment of the poor."*

Knowing nowhere else to turn, she called our church and received financial aid. Felicia was shown mercy—undeserved, unearned grace—in her time of need. By the work of God's Spirit, she apprehended this, and it made her both humble and appreciative. Shortly after, Felicia requested to be matched with a new mentor—a relationship that still continues two years later. With that mentor's help, Felicia secured her GED, moved out of public housing, and successfully completed our job training program. She is currently employed in a medical clinic.

As I mulled over Felicia's story, I realized that, had I been in charge of the church's benevolence fund at the time, I would have vetoed the idea of helping her out of her jam with the electric company. I'd have argued that saying no was necessary, that assistance would be merely a handout likely to enable Felicia to continue in her self-destructive habits. Better to have her feel the consequences of her behavior, I would have argued, and perhaps be jolted by them onto a healthier course.

I was forced to admit that the church's demonstration of mercy was crucial to the remarkable progress Felicia has made in the past three years. A "tough love" refusal back then might have pushed her to better behavior, but it might also have turned her off completely to Christianity. The gospel's claim to offer "undeserved favor to sinners" has become a more plausible idea to Felicia, for she can remember when the congregation showed her such mercy.

Ethical Calculus

Felicia's testimony filled my thoughts as I stood alongside Interstate 64, looking into Jacqueline's weather-beaten and lined face. I didn't have enough information to judge her deserts. I didn't want to enable her dysfunctional lifestyle, yet I was singularly unable to convince her of a better path. Her personal fear of shelters, and her obvious mental limits, prevented rational discussion. And my refusal to help her would not leave her in circumstances that would force her to avail herself of the Salvation Army. After all, she and her "old man" had been managing several days without me. So I "helped" her—fully aware that perhaps at some level I was also hurting her. The ethical calculus in this circumstance was complicated: the aid and friendliness I showed her for a few days, I pray, offered her some small touch of God's mercy. She knew I was a Christian, for we talked of it and of the things of Christ.

Additionally, in my exchange with Jacqueline, I felt God was working on me. As we waited in the grocery store check-out line, I recalled the words "Give to the one who asks from you" (Matt. 5:42). As I killed time in the Family Dollar, Michael Card's lyrics echoed in my head:

> In His distressing disguise,
> He waits for us to surmise
> That when we take care of the poorest of them;
> We've really done it to Him.

I don't intend to give any more handouts soon. I've seen too often the harm they do and heard too many sad stories from other front-lines practitioners whose efforts to transform people's lives are hampered by naive donors practicing "random acts of kindness." I hope all compassionate people will read Payne's book on expectant giving. But I also pray that we'll be sensitive to the Holy Spirit's prompting and allow some space for grace.

Charity Means You Don't Pick and Choose

by Patricia O'Hara

About the author: *Patricia O'Hara is a freelance writer in Strasburg, Pennsylvania.*

"If you're not going to eat that, little boy, I will," said the man sitting on the sidewalk to my son, who was holding a doggie bag of restaurant leftovers. It was the first time my son had ever seen a homeless person. He was 5 years old, and we were spending the weekend visiting museums in Washington, D.C. It was a March night of unusually raw weather—not a night to be sitting on a cold, hard sidewalk. I tightened my grasp on my son's hand as I made eye contact with the man.

"Spare Anything, Ma'am?"

My son looked up at me uneasily, so I left him with my husband and went over to the man, dollar extended. He thanked me and asked my son again for his doggie bag. I motioned him over, nodding my assurances. "I didn't finish my steak sandwich," my son told him proudly, as he handed the man his bag. The man thanked him and said, "Be good to your mommy."

At just that moment a father and his two teenage sons walked past and, without breaking his stride, barked out: "It'd be better if they got a job!"

I was startled by the intensity of the man's disapproval, but I, too, have had doubts about offering handouts to the homeless. Under the watchful eyes of my child, I chose the action that I hoped would speak to my son about the principles of charity I hold dear, but the truth is, my decision to give has seldom been so clear-cut.

Like most people, I'm more comfortable giving when the people on the receiving end are anonymous. I happily participate in the clothing drives sponsored by my son's school, and I drop my spare change in the big metal kettle at the mall, where a man dressed like Santa Claus rings his bell and smiles at shoppers.

Patricia O'Hara, "Charity Means You Don't Pick and Choose," *Newsweek*, December 23, 2002, p. 13.

Giving directly to the street person shambling across my pathway—well, that's another matter. Hollywood tends to portray the homeless as lovable rogues (think Eddie Murphy in *Trading Places*), but in real life, the person asking for money is often suffering the effects of mental illness or addiction. I'm not proud to admit it, but even the few seconds it takes to look the other person in the eye, extend my hand and offer some change can feel like more of a connection than I want to make.

I've heard the intellectual arguments against giving handouts: the money will be used to buy drugs or alcohol, handouts breed dependency, giving money discourages the homeless from going to shelters. I don't want to undermine the efforts of the mental-health professionals who work to get the homeless off the streets. But what I know in my head doesn't square with what I feel in my heart. Pretending that people don't exist and withholding a couple of quarters or a dollar bill feels like the wrong thing to do.

Several years after our encounter with the homeless man in Washington, my son and I visited New York City. As we walked down the street, a thin, drugged-out young man approached us and asked us for change. It was midtown at midday, so there was nothing particularly threatening about the circumstances. Nevertheless, the man was, by anyone's standards, unsavory-looking with his dirty clothes and unhealthy skin. I passed him by. Half a block later, my son stopped walking and asked: "Why didn't you give him anything?" I fumbled through a rationale about how we hadn't had time to stop and why we couldn't possibly give to everyone. My son interrupted and said, "Yeah, I don't think you should give money to people like that."

"People Like That"

In his words and his tone of voice were echoes of the man who told the panhandler to get a job. I had shown my son that it was acceptable to classify people as the deserving and the undeserving poor.

[In the spring of 2002] I traveled to London to do some work-related research. Each day on the way to the library, I passed a group of homeless men lying on the steps of St. Pancras Old Church. Perhaps spending time in one of Charles Dickens's old neighborhoods set me thinking about his righteous anger at society's neglect of its poor. Or maybe I finally accepted that I'm in no position—and who is?—to judge another person's worthiness of a small act of kindness. Whatever the reason, I decided that I would always give when asked, even when it means weathering the sidelong glances of those who think I'm a fool or worse.

My son is now a teenager and will have to decide for himself if and how he'll give to the poor. For all of my inconsistencies, I hope that I've taught him that it's better to set the needle of his compass to the magnetic pull of kindness than to contempt. But time alone will tell.

Organizations to Contact

The editors have compiled the following list of organizations concerned with the issues debated in this book. The descriptions are derived from materials provided by the organizations. All have publications or information available for interested readers. The list was compiled on the date of publication of the present volume; the information provided here may change. Be aware that many organizations take several weeks or longer to respond to inquiries, so allow as much time as possible.

American Enterprise Institute for Public Policy Research (AEI)
1150 Seventeenth St. NW, Washington, DC 20036
(202) 862-5800 • fax: (202) 862-7178
e-mail: info@aei.org • website: www.aei.org

The institute is dedicated to preserving and strengthening the foundations of freedom—limited government, private enterprise, vital cultural and political institutions, and a strong foreign policy and national defense—through scholarly research, open debate, and publications. AEI research covers economics and trade; social welfare; government tax, spending, regulatory and legal policies; domestic politics; international affairs; and defense and foreign policies. The institute publishes dozens of books and hundreds of articles and reports each year as well as a policy magazine, *America Enterprise.*

Brookings Institution
1775 Massachusetts Ave. NW, Washington, DC 20036-2188
(202) 797-6000 • fax: (202) 797-6004
e-mail: brookinfo@brook.edu • website: www.brookings.edu

The institution is devoted to nonpartisan research, education, and publication in economics, government, foreign policy, and the social sciences. Its principal purposes are to aid in the development of sound public policies and to promote public understanding of issues of national importance. It publishes the quarterly journal the *Brookings Review*, which periodically includes articles on poverty, and numerous books, including *The Urban Underclass.*

Cato Institute
1000 Massachusetts Ave. NW, Washington, DC 20001-5403
(202) 842-0200 • fax: (202) 842-3490
e-mail: cato@cato.org • website: www.cato.org

The institute is a libertarian public policy research organization that advocates limited government. It has published a variety of literature concerning poverty and housing in its quarterly *Cato Journal* and in its Policy Analysis series.

Center for Law and Social Policy (CLASP)
1015 15th St. NW, Suite 400, Washington, DC 20005
(202) 906-8000 • fax: (202) 842-2885
website: www.clasp.org

CLASP is a national nonprofit organization that seeks to improve the economic conditions of low-income families with children. The center analyzes federal and state policies and practices in the areas of welfare reform and workforce development and produces materials designed to explain the implications of these policies and practices. Available on the CLASP website are numerous individual publications on issues related to family economic security and civil legal assistance.

Center of Concern
3700 13th St. NE, Washington, DC 20017
(202) 635-2757 • fax: (202) 832-9494
e-mail: coc@igc.apc.org • website: www.coc.org/coc/

Center of Concern engages in social analysis, theological reflection, policy advocacy, and public education on issues of justice and peace. Its programs and writings include subjects such as international development, women's roles, economic alternatives, and a theology based on justice for all peoples. It publishes the bimonthly newsletter *Center Focus* as well as numerous papers and books, including *Opting for the Poor: A Challenge for North Americans.*

Center on Budget and Policy Priorities
820 First St. NE, Suite 510, Washington, DC 20002
(202) 408-1080 • fax: (202) 408-1056
e-mail: center@center.cbpp.org • website: www.cbpp.org

The center promotes better public understanding of the impact of federal and state governmental spending policies and programs primarily affecting low- and moderate-income Americans. It acts as a research center and information clearinghouse for the media, national and local organizations, and individuals. The center publishes numerous fact sheets, articles, and reports, including *The Safety Net Delivers: The Effects of Government Benefit Programs in Reducing Poverty.*

Children's Defense Fund (CDF)
25 E St. NW, Washington, DC 20001
(202) 628-8787
e-mail: cdfinfo@childrensdefense.org • website: www.childrensdefense.org

CDF works to promote the interests of children in America. It pays particular attention to the needs of poor, minority, and disabled children. Its publications include *The State of America's Children* and *Wasting America's Future: The Children's Defense Fund's Report on the Costs of Child Poverty.*

Coalition on Human Needs
1000 Wisconsin Ave. NW, Washington, DC 20007
(202) 342-0726 • fax: (202) 338-1856
e-mail: chn@chn.org

The coalition is a federal advocacy organization that works in such areas as federal budget and tax policy, housing, education, health care, and public assistance. It lobbies for adequate federal funding for welfare, Medicaid, and other social services. Its publications include *How the Poor Would Remedy Poverty*, the *Directory of National Human Needs Organizations*, and the biweekly legislative newsletter the *Human Needs Report.*

Co-operative Housing Association of Ontario (CHAO)
2 Berkeley St., Suite 207, Toronto, ON M5A 2W3 Canada
(800) 268-2537 • fax: (416) 366-3876

CHAO is a provincial housing advocacy group that works with other housing and homeless organizations throughout Ontario to develop educational and political campaigns. It maintains a housing research library with resource materials on housing issues in Canada and around the world. CHAO commissions and publishes studies on a variety of housing issues. Its publications include the monthly *Dispatches* and *Co-op Memo*, the biweekly *Resource Group Memo*, the quarterly newsletter *Co-op Bulletin*, and the semiannual *Cross Sections.*

Economic Policy Institute
1660 L St. NW, Suite 1200, Washington, DC 20036
(202) 775-8810 • (800) 374-4844 (publications)
e-mail: blustig@epinet.org • website: www.epinet.org

The institute was established in 1986 to pursue research and public education to help define a new economic strategy for the United States. Its goal is to identify policies that can provide prosperous, fair, and balanced economic growth. It publishes numerous policy studies, briefing papers, and books, including the titles *State of Working America* and *Declining American Incomes and Living Standards.*

Heritage Foundation
214 Massachusetts Ave. NE, Washington, DC 20002-4999
(202) 546-4400 • fax: (202) 546-8328
e-mail: info@heritage.org • website: www.heritage.org

The foundation is a public policy research institute dedicated to the principles of free competitive enterprise, limited government, individual liberty, and a strong national defense. The foundation publishes the monthly newsletter *Insider* and *Heritage Today*, a newsletter published six times per year, as well as various reports and journals.

Homes for the Homeless (HFH)
36 Cooper Square, Sixth Fl., New York, NY 10003
(212) 529-5252 • fax: (212) 529-7698
e-mail: info@homesforthehomeless.com • website:
www.homesforthehomeless.com

HFH strives to reduce homelessness by providing families with the education and training they need to build independent lives. Participating families are housed in residential educational training centers, where they learn job, literacy, and parenting skills. Participants are also counseled on substance abuse and domestic violence. HFH publishes the reports *The New Poverty: A Generation of Homeless Families* and *Job Readiness: Crossing the Threshold from Homelessness to Employment.*

National Alliance to End Homelessness
1518 K St. NW, Suite 206, Washington, DC 20005
(202) 638-1526M • fax: (202) 638-4664
e-mail: naeh@naeh.org • website: www.naeh.org

The alliance is a national organization composed of state and local nonprofit agencies, corporations, and individuals committed to the ideal that no American should have to be homeless. Its goal is to end homelessness by changing federal policy and by helping its local members serve more homeless people. Its publications include *What You Can Do to Help the Homeless* and the monthly newsletter *Alliance.*

National Coalition for the Homeless
1012 Fourteenth St. NW, Suite 600, Washington, DC 20005-3471
(202) 737-6444 • fax: (202) 737-6445
website: www.nationalhomeless.org

The coalition is a national advocacy network of activists, homeless persons, service providers, and others committed to ending homelessness through public education, policy advocacy, grassroots organizing, and technical assistance. It lobbies for government programs to help the homeless, conducts research, and works as a clearinghouse on information about the homeless. In addition to many pamphlets and reports, it publishes the monthly newsletter *Safety Network.*

National Student Campaign Against Hunger and Homelessness (NSCAHH)
233 N. Pleasant Ave., Amherst, MA 01002
(413) 253-6417 • fax: (413) 255-6435
e-mail: nscah@aol.com • website: www.nscahh.org

NSCAHH is a network of college and high school students, educators, and community leaders who work to fight hunger and homelessness in the United States and around the world. Its mission is to create a generation of student/community activists who will explore and understand the root causes of poverty and who will initiate positive change through service and action. It publishes the quarterly newsletter *Students Making a Difference* as well as numerous manuals, fact sheets, and handbooks.

Poverty and Race Research Action Council (PRRAC)
1711 Connecticut Ave. NW, No. 207, Washington, DC 20009
(202) 387-9887 • fax: (202) 387-0764
e-mail: prrac@aol.com • website: www.prrac.org

PRRAC was established by civil rights, antipoverty, and legal services groups. It works to develop antiracism and antipoverty, strategies and provides funding for research projects that support advocacy work. It publishes the bimonthly newsletter *Poverty & Race.*

Progressive Policy Institute (PPI)
316 Pennsylvania Ave. SE, Suite 555, Washington, DC 20003
(202) 547-0001
e-mail: webmaster@dlcppi.org

PPI develops policy alternatives to the conventional liberal-conservative political debate. It advocates social policies that move beyond merely maintaining the poor to liberating them from poverty and dependency. Its publications include *Microenterprise: Human Reconstruction in America's Inner Cities* and *Social Service Vouchers: Bringing Choice and Competition to Social Services.*

Bibliography

Books

Randy Albelda and Ann Withorn, eds.	*Lost Ground: Welfare Reform, Poverty, and Beyond.* Cambridge, MA: South End Press, 2002.
Douglas J. Besharov, ed.	*Family Well-Being After Welfare Reform.* Somerset, NJ: Transaction, 2003.
Martha Burt et al.	*Helping America's Homeless: Emergency Shelter or Affordable Housing.* Washington, DC: Urban Institute Press, 2001.
Chuck Collins and Felice Yeskel	*Economic Apartheid in America: A Primer on Economic Inequality and Insecurity.* New York: New Press, 2000.
Dalton Conley, ed.	*Wealth and Poverty in America: A Reader.* Malden, MA: Blackwell, 2002.
Sheldon Danziger and Robert H. Haveman, eds.	*Poverty.* Cambridge, MA: Harvard University Press, 2002.
Todd DePastino	*Citizen Hobo: How a Century of Homelessness Shaped America.* Chicago: University of Chicago Press, 2003.
Rosemarie T. Downer	*Homelessness and Its Consequences: Impact on Children's Psychological Well-Being.* New York: Routledge, 2001.
Barbara Ehrenreich	*Nickel and Dimed: On (Not) Getting By in America.* New York: Henry Holt, 2001.
D. Stanley Eitzen et al.	*Experiencing Poverty: Voices from the Bottom.* Belmont, CA: Wadsworth, 2002.
Sharon Hays	*Flat Broke with Children: Women in the Age of Welfare Reform.* New York: Oxford University Press, 2003.
Lori Holyfield	*Moving Up and Out: Poverty, Education, and the Single Parent Family.* Philadephia: Temple University Press, 2002.
Kim Hopper	*Reckoning with Homelessness.* Ithaca, NY: Cornell University Press, 2002.
James Jennings	*Welfare Reform and the Revitalization of Inner City Neighborhoods.* East Lansing: Michigan State University Press, 2003.

Poverty and the Homeless

Joanna Lipper	*Growing Up Fast.* New York: Picador, 2003.
Marjorie Mayers	*Street Kids and Streetscapes: Panhandling, Politics, and Prophecies.* New York: Peter Lang, 2001.
George S. McGovern	*The Third Freedom: Ending Hunger in Our Time.* New York: Rowman & Littlefield, 2002.
Lawrence M. Mead	*Government Matters: Welfare Reform in Wisconsin.* Princeton, NJ: Princeton University Press, 2004.
Michelle Miller-Adams	*Owning Up: Poverty, Assets, and the American Dream.* Washington, DC: Brookings Institution Press, 2002.
David Neumark	*How Living Wage Laws Affect Low-Wage Workers and Low-Income Families.* San Francisco: Public Policy Institute of California, 2002.
Benjamin I. Page and James Roy Simmons	*What Government Can Do: Dealing with Poverty and Inequality.* Chicago: University of Chicago Press, 2002.
James T. Patterson	*America's Struggle Against Poverty in the Twentieth Century.* Cambridge, MA: Harvard University Press, 2000.
Sanford F. Schram, Joe Soss, and Richard C. Fording, eds.	*Race and the Politics of Welfare Reform.* Ann Arbor: University of Michigan Press, 2003.
Loretta Schwartz-Nobel	*Growing Up Empty: The Hunger Epidemic in America.* New York: HarperCollins, 2002.
Steven Shafarman	*We the People: Healing Our Democracy and Saving Our World.* Van Nuys, CA: Gain, 2001.
Holly Sklar et al.	*Raise the Floor: Wages and Policies That Work for Us All.* New York: Ms. Foundation for Women, 2001.

Periodicals

Caralee J. Adams	"A Time of Compassion," *Better Homes and Gardens,* December 1999.
Willie Baptist and Mary Bricker-Jenkins	"A New Era in the Struggle Against Poverty," *Dollars and Sense,* September/October 2002.
Deepak Bhargava and Joan Kuriansky	"Drawing the Line on Poverty," *Washington Post National Weekly Edition,* September 23–29, 2002.
Albert Bliss	"Homeless Man Interviews Himself," *Harper's Magazine,* September 2001.
Charmion Browne	"When Shelter Feels Like a Prison," *New York Time,* August 13, 2002.
W. Michael Cox and Richard Alm	"Why Decry the Wealth Gap?" *New York Times,* January 24, 2000.

Bibliography

Economist	"America's Great Achievement: Welfare Reform," August 25, 2001.
Peter Edelman	"Poverty and Welfare: Does Compassionate Conservatism Have a Heart?" *Albany Law Review*, Spring 2001.
Barbara Ehrenreich	"America's Torrent of Need," *Los Angeles Times*, August 5, 2001.
Fred Gaboury	"Homelessness Rises Across the Nation," *People's Weekly World*, January 12, 2002.
Lawrence E. Harrison	"The Cultural Roots of Poverty," *Wall Street Journal*, July 13, 1999.
Ron Haskins	"Giving Is NOT Enough," *Brookings Review*, Summer 2001.
Robert V. Hess	"Helping People Off the Streets: Real Solutions to Urban Homelessness," *USA Today* (Magazine), January 2000.
Jacob G. Hornberger	"The Minimum Wage: Enemy of the Poor," *Liberty*, July 1999.
Fidelis Iyebote	"How Poverty-Stricken Is the U.S.?" *World & I*, January 2000.
Patricia Ann Lamoureux	"Improving Welfare Reform," *America*, April 8, 2002.
Ed Loring	"Housing Comes First," *The Other Side*, May/June 2002.
Ed Marciniak	"Recalculating Poverty," *Commonweal*, January 28, 2000.
Marci McDonald	"Homeless in Silicon Valley," *Redbook*, November 2000.
Jack Newfield	"How the Other Half Still Lives: In the Shadow of Wealth, New York's Poor Increase," *Nation*, March 17, 2003.
Margot Patterson	"Hungry in America," *National Catholic Reporter*, February 15, 2002.
Robert Pear	"Number of People Living in Poverty Increases in U.S.," *New York Times*, August 25, 2002.
Robert E. Rector	"Not So Poor: The Luxury of American Poverty," *National Review*, October 25, 1999.
Holly Sklar	"$5.15 an Hour Just Doesn't Add Up," *Democratic Left*, Spring 2002.
Thomas Sowell	"Leftists Use Poor as Means to an End," *Human Events*, December 15, 2000.
Joel Stein	"The Real Face of Homelessness: More than Ever, It Is Mothers with Kids Who Are Ending Up on the Streets," *Time*, January 20, 2003.
Peter Stock	"Poverty on Paper: Claims of Rising Child Destitution Do Not Hold Up to Scrutiny," *Report Newsmagazine*, February 16, 2002.
Mark Stricherz	"How Faith-Based Charities Can Work: The Success of Covenant House," *Crisis*, September 2002.

Michael Tanner	"Welfare Reform: How Successful?" *World & I*, October 2001.
Jim Tull	"Shall the Poor Always Be with Us?" *The Other Side*, May/June 2002.
Jim Wallis	"Amid Prosperity, Many Kinds of Poverty," *Los Angeles Times*, August 15, 2000.

Index